Praise for *Chienke's Motl*
Ce

MW01610566

"This is a heart-warming, and occasionally heart-breaking memoir of Motl and Chienke Sivak ... Though each one alone or together faced devastations such as pograms and World War I and the loss of a child, they drew tremendous strength from their activism in movements expressing the Utopian Socialist-Zionist ideals of Kibbutz. This pioneering spirit never left them regardless of their circumstances or where they lived : Eastern Europe, Canada or pre-State Israel. Their unwavering principles, initiative, compassion and care are testimonies to how ordinary people choose to do good... Their son who edited (the) memoirs added his gloss: Jacob's Commentary. In it he provides the historical context to many of the events or personalities described, literary or philological sources to unusual words or songs mentioned. "An important document, originally written in Yiddish, for those interested in the history of Jewish emigration to Montreal in the 1920s,"

Leah Cohen
Library and Archives Canada

" an intimate and very personal history of a generation that must be remembered."
Professor Jack Pasternak, University of Waterloo.

"What is most striking to this reviewer is the emerging and developing personality of each of the authors, as much as is their unique and textured story line. Few and far between do tales of true pioneers come so clearly and forcefully to us as this memoir did to me... a testimony to the power of words – in particular those that they chose to describe a remarkable sojourn on this planet merely one generation ago."

Daniel Maoz
Research Associate
Department of Religion
Concordia University

Chienke's Motl and Motl's Chienke

by Max Sivak and Jennie Sivak

Edited with commentary by Jacob G. Sivak

Published by
Mantua Books
Brantford, Ontario N3T 6J9
Vancouver B.C. V6K 4C4
Email: Mantua2003@Hotmail.com

Library and Archives Canada Cataloguing in Publication

Sivak, Max, 1909-2002
    Chienke's Motl and Motl's Chienke : a twentieth century story / Max Sivak
and Jennie Sivak ; edited with a commentary by Jacob G. Sivak.

ISBN 978-0-9734065-6-6

    1. Sivak, Max, 1909-2002. 2. Sivak, Jennie, 1910-1996. 3. Jews--Québec
(Province)--Montréal--Biography. I. Sivak, Jennie, 1910-1996 II. Sivak, Jacob
G., 1944- III. Title.

FC2947.26.S59A3 2011   971.4'280049240092   C2011-904152-9

Foreword

I tend to think of this book as my father's book. More precisely, this book is actually my parents' book because in the initial stages both my father and mother were involved in the writing. On the other hand, the driving force for its creation as an English text was really my father.

The book was initially written in Yiddish as a memoir by the two of them, and its length included material from the early periods of their lives to the later ones. It has a long history going back 15 or 20 years, but only in manuscript form. The early Yiddish version was typed by a sympathetic friend of my parents whose name I do not recall. There was probably more than one Yiddish version, but I'm not sure, for while my parents made sure that I attended a parochial school that taught Hebrew, I never did receive any formal Yiddish education. As a result, I can't decipher the various bits and pieces of the Yiddish manuscript left by my parents after they passed away. My understanding of spoken Yiddish, which is pretty good, stems simply from hearing my parents speak it at home. However, I can only speak it very poorly and reading of anything, other than newspaper headlines by sounding out the Hebrew letters, is quite impossible.

At some point my father realized that his (their) memoir would have to be translated into English if it was going to have any chance of being passed down to the next generation of family members and beyond. His next step was to translate it himself, very laboriously and by hand, into a crude form of English and hope that someone would come along and help by doing the editing. As will be seen in the actual chapters themselves, my father had little formal education in any language. However, as was the case for many of his generation, he managed to educate himself. He did have a variety of exposures to religious and Yiddish/Hebrew education during his early years and of course his years in Palestine led to a fluency in Hebrew. In fact, this was also largely true for my mother, especially since she too spent several years in Palestine during the 1930s. However, while he could read and speak English very well, his ability to write it and spell it accurately was poor.

As I mentioned earlier, the first version of this memoir was written in Yiddish, by both of my parents and, as the name and the introduction indicate, it was intended to be a cooperative project for the two of them in their elder years. However, I suspect, as also already noted, that the idea was primarily my father's and it is possible that my mother went along with it as a means of ensuring that he was occupied. Moreover, my mother's penmanship was very good, something she took great pride in, while my father's was terrible. As a consequence, my father relied on my mother to rewrite the work as he went along so that it could be read and typed into acceptable Yiddish. This is not meant to diminish my mother's role. She certainly must have written the second chapter, which deals entirely with her early life, and I'm sure that she contributed a great deal to the rest of the Yiddish version.

The writing continued over several years; after all, it was a labor of love and not a way to make a living. As time went on, my mother became ill and the project was gradually taken over entirely by my father. There is no question that the effort to translate the work into English was his, and the evidence is provided by the many pages of handwritten rough translation consisting mostly of very poorly spelled English interspersed with words and phrases in Yiddish or Hebrew.

So, now we come to the point where my father had translated the first three chapters of his and my mother's story and was casting about for editing help. His first thought would have been to see if either or both of his children, my sister or myself, would help. Then there were nephews and nieces and grandchildren to consider. However, we were all busy and involved in living our own lives and the thought of adding a new task that involved deciphering and then editing someone else's thoughts just didn't sound very appealing, no matter how highly we thought of him as a father, uncle or grandfather. I should mention that my father was not one to directly ask for help. Rather, his approach was to tell us what he was up to and then hope that we would offer to help. Well, someone did take him up on it and that someone was my cousin Irving. Irving is the son of Chaike, my father's youngest sister and the sibling closest to him in age, my father being the youngest of a family with seven children. Irving is the only cousin I have who is about my age (actually, he's a year older).

Irving, who grew up in the United States, mostly in Detroit, was a psychology professor at the University of Connecticut (he is currently a professor at the University of Hull, in the UK). On one of his periodic visits to Montreal he must have agreed to help with the book project, perhaps because his mother had done something similar in writing and publishing her own memoirs in Yiddish. In any case, Irving did type and edit the first chapter, which includes a brief introduction and the early years of my father's life. At this point, I felt that I had to participate as well and so I edited and typed the next chapter, the one dealing with my mother's early years. My father and mother were pleased to get my help and I suspect that my father hoped to entice other family members to deal with the subsequent chapters. However, since I enjoyed the editing once I started, and since additional family volunteers didn't materialize, it was left to me to edit the remaining six chapters that constitute this book.

After starting with a description of how my parents met in Montreal in 1925, the first chapter of the memoir describes my father's early years in the Ukraine, the tragedy that befell his family during the post-World War I civil war between the red forces and the white groups in Russia, his family's flight to Bessarabia (Romania at that time, Moldavia today) as refugees and their subsequent immigration to Canada. The second deals with my mother's childhood in Lithuania, the trials and tribulations faced by her mother and siblings during World War I and the family's post-war migration to Montreal. The focus of Chapter Three is the description of the various Zionist youth organizations that existed in Montreal during the 1920s and 1930s, my parent's involvement in them, and my father's experience as a migrant worker during the wheat harvest in Western Canada. The western adventure was intended to provide farming experience as a training exercise for future pioneering work in Palestine. This experience was a life-defining experience that my father referred to repeatedly to friends and relatives, including me. The next chapter, the fourth, describes my father's immigration and, later my mother's, to Palestine, and their efforts to familiarize themselves with the kibbutz movement as it existed in the 1930s. It also goes into my parent's disillusionment with kibbutz life and their decision to leave. Chapter Five deals with my parents' efforts to survive in Haifa after leaving the kibbutz with my sister, their later return to Montreal shortly before the outbreak of

World War II, and their difficulties in finding employment and re-establishing themselves in a society they had left behind. The sixth chapter describes the Adath Israel Congregation, including synagogue and school, the institution which my father served as superintendent for thirteen years and the final chapter deals with my father's experience as an installment merchant during the final period of his working life.

While I have enjoyed the editing, my initial reason for doing it was to please my parents (well, mainly my father) and to help provide a memoir that might be of some value to members of our family with an interest in family history. However, as I progressed further into the editing, it began to be clear that at least some of the material portrayed could be of more general interest. For example, the description of the development of the early Zionist youth movements in Montreal provides an interesting historical perspective on an important aspect of Canadian Jewish history. The same could be said for the material describing my father's experience as a migrant worker in the wheat fields of Western Canada, which he and a friend undertook to prepare themselves for life as pioneers in Palestine (Eretz Yisrael). Also, my father's description of his work as an installment merchant, or customer pedlar, describes a business niche occupied mainly by Montreal Jews during the period that preceded the credit card era and is, to my knowledge, a topic that has not attracted much, if any, literary attention.

I had always been close to my parents, both in my younger and adult years, and the editing project brought us even closer. After my mother passed away I continued to proceed with my father alone. My writing skills have been honed mainly by over 38 years of scientific writing and editing. Editing my father's work wasn't too different from working through a graduate student's research thesis and improving it without altering the writer's message or style. This book is essentially an historical memoir, and while I don't have a formal background in the study of history, I have followed and read about History and Jewish History in particular for my entire adult life. If during the editing I came across a name place or an event I wasn't familiar with I consulted the books in my personal library, including the Encyclopedia Judaica. On occasion Google or Wikipedia were useful sources of information.

Once my father passed away the project was placed on hold. In fact, my father's translating effort petered out even before he died. He translated two more chapters dealing mainly with more recent family history and their more recent nature meant that they were of lesser interest to me, particularly because my memory of the same events did not always coincide precisely with my father's. When my father was still alive the thought of publishing the memoir cropped up from time to time. I approached the Wilfrid Laurier University Press on his behalf when I heard that there was an interest in immigrant memoirs. This interest extended to including the chapters that were edited to that point in a university archive, but not to publication. My father was delighted that there was at least some interest. On another occasion I came across an advertisement from a western Canadian literary magazine asking for submissions dealing with western Jewish themes. On his behalf, I submitted the chapter that included my father's experience as a migrant worker on the prairies. Nevertheless, this led to a polite rejection.

Now, some eight years after my father's death, I have given the matter more thought with the idea of adding to and annotating the chapters with my own perspective on the events they describe. For example, I thought that the chapter dealing with my mother's early life in Lithuania brings up an interesting point pertaining to the relationship between the Jewish inhabitants of Lithuania and the German soldiers who invaded and controlled the area for a few years during World War I. This exposure to German soldiers by East European Jewry was to lead to tragic consequences barely twenty years later, insofar as the Holocaust is concerned. Similarly, I felt that some explanation and amplification as to the immigration of German Jews to Palestine during the early years of the Nazi regime, and in particular, the Transfer Agreement between the Jewish Agency of Palestine and German Government, would be an interesting and helpful addition to my father's description of kibbutz life during the 1930s.

My own background is much less exciting or precarious, to my mind, than the experiences that my parents went through. I grew up safe and secure in Montreal. My early life did have its peculiarities in that for most of the first six years of my life my family and I lived in an apartment located in the synagogue complex that my father tended to in his job as superintendent. When I was about seven we moved out of the synagogue into a nearby apartment, and when I was eight my father left his synagogue job to become an independent businessman as an installment merchant/customer pedlar. At that point, he purchased a car, our family's first, to be used mainly for his business but also for family visits and short vacation trips.

I attended a private Jewish parochial school until the completion of grade nine. The school provided Hebrew and English instruction on a 50/50 basis, with the Hebrew component consisting mainly of secular topics, although, as I already pointed out, no Yiddish. Students could receive some traditional orthodox religious instruction by attending a children's service on Saturdays, something I did rather infrequently.

I cannot think of any particular point of interest to relate that would be much different than the experience of any other Canadian boy growing up in the late forties and early fifties, except to note that I sensed at an early age an element of concern and unease on Jewish matters. This stemmed both from home and school. I recall an early school assembly when the principal referred to the "six million martyrs of the Holocaust," my first inkling of the enormous tragedy that befell the Jewish people just a few years earlier. Once I was old enough to understand a little of what was going on around me I became aware of terms used to describe evildoers such as Nazis, Germans, reds, communists (this was the time of the Korean War) and I recall quizzing my father on their meaning. My parents were fortunate in that they didn't experience the Holocaust directly. However, my mother's eldest brother, Hirshel, and his wife and children were murdered in Lithuania during this time and I know that my mother thought of them frequently, particularly on occasions such as family events and Passover seders.

I was aware of the formation of the state of Israel at an early age, and while I knew that this was a good thing, I was also aware that Israel's existence was insecure and not a sure thing, a feeling that continued until I was considerably older in 1967 when the Six Day War took place, and which continues somewhat today. When I was seven or eight years old I learned from somewhere that Jerusalem, at least the old city, was not at that point in time a part of Israel. When I quizzed my mother on why this was the case, she replied, somewhat wistfully, that it was still possible to look into the old city from the site of David's tomb on Mount Zion. I mention these early observations to add some of my own background to that of my parent's as I became somewhat more than an editor of their memoirs.

The editing I became involved in to help my father in his project produced a special bond between us, one that I think of as being similar to that portrayed by Phillip Roth in Paternity, a touching biographical story describing the author's interaction with **his** father during the latter's final years. My father read Roth's book and enjoyed it very much, and I think that he too felt that **our** interaction was similar to that portrayed by Roth. I suppose that in part this book gives me an opportunity to continue the partnership that developed between my father and me during the last few years of his life.

I have annotated the seven chapters, which follow with my own thoughts and observations, and I have made an effort to provide an historical context to the events that are described. My annotations are headed as Jacob's Commmentary. They are written in the first person. When I am mentioned in the text of these memoirs, usually by the diminutive form of my Yiddish name as Yankale, as in the later chapters, I am refered to in the third person.

The memoirs and my annotations include a number of Hebrew and Yiddish terms that may not be widely familiar. I have added some explanatory material to the text or as footnotes, where possible, and a glossary of terms follows this prologue.

I would like to acknowledge the contribution of my cousin, Irving Kirsch, who edited the first English version of Chapter 1, as well as my daughter, Alisa Sivak, who provided editing assistance during the final stages. Thanks are also due to Jack Pasternak who suggested that I provide my own commentary to my father's writings and to Paul Socken and Daniel Maoz who read and corrected earlier versions and made suggestions. Finally, thank you to Ami Dovrat for tracking down the song that my father referred to in Chapter 4.

J. Sivak, June 2011
Waterloo

Glossary

Adath	Congregation or assembly (Hebrew).
Aliyah	The act of immigrating (going up, or ascending) to Israel (Hebrew).
Balabusta	A good homemaker (Yiddish, derived from the Hebrew baal ha-bayit).
Bar Mitzvah	A coming of age event that takes place when a Jewish boy becomes 13 years of age and is responsible for his actions, under Jewish law (Hebrew).
Bemazal tov	With good luck (Hebrew).
Bima	Raised platform ("high place") from which the Torah is read in a synagogue (Hebrew).
Bris	Ritual circumcision of boys, performed normally on the eighth day after birth (Yiddish).
Bubbe	Grandmother (Yiddish).
Cheder	Traditional elementary school teaching the basics of Judaism and Hebrew. Classes were usually held in the teacher's home.
Challes	Braided egg bread associated with Sabbath and Holiday meals.
Chalutz	A pioneer, or early Jewish immigrant to Palestine (Hebrew).
Chalutziut	Zionist pioneering.
Chaver	Friend, comrade (Hebrew).

Dunam	Ottoman term for a unit of area equivalent to 1000 square meters.
Eretz Yisrael	Land of Israel (Biblical Hebrew).
Galut (the)	The Diaspora (exile).
Hadar HaCarmel	A neighbourhood of Haifa, once the commercial centre, located between the upper (Carmel) and lower (Port) areas of the city.
Haganah	The primary pre-State of Israel paramilitary force (Haganah).
Halacha	Jewish religious law (Hebrew).
Hapoal	The worker (Hebrew).
Hashomer	An early Jewish paramilitary defense force in Palestine. Led to the foundation of the youth movement, *Hashomar Hatzair (*Hebrew for "the young guards").
Histadrut	General Federation of Labour, a major economic and political force in Israel.
Kaddish	An important prayer (in Aramaic) said frequently in the Jewish liturgy, and specifically by mourners. The expression "saying kaddish" refers to mourning.
Lag BaOmer	A holiday on the 33rd day in the counting of the Omer. The "49 days of the Omer" refers to the period between the time when the Jews were freed from slavery in Egypt and the giving of the Torah on Mount Sinai, on Shavuot. Restrictions on celebrations such as weddings, parties, etc., which are not

permitted during the period of the counting of the Omer, are lifted for this day.

Landsman	Someone from the old country (Yiddish).
Kibbutz	A collective community in Israel, originally agricultural, that combines socialism and Zionism.
Kinneret	The Sea of Galilee. The name is commonly believed to be derived from the Hebrew for harp, referring to the shape of this body of water (Hebrew).
Kol Nidre	Prayer said at the evening service at the start of Yom Kippur (the Day of Atonement) (Aramaic).
L'chaim	A Jewish toast, literally "to life" (Hebrew and Yiddish).
Mechitza	Divider separating men and woman sections in an orthodox synagogue.
Megilla	Book of Esther, which is read during the holiday of Purim.
Mikvah	Ritual bathhouse (Hebrew).
Mikveh Israel	The first Jewish agricultural school in Palestine.
Minyan	A quorum of ten (men, in the orthodox tradition) required for public prayer.
Misnagdim	The intellectuals who opposed Hassidism and upheld traditional Jewish scholarship (Hebrew).
Mitzvah	Good deed (Hebrew).

Moshav	A cooperative agricultural community in Israel in which farms are privately owned.
Oneg Sahabbat	Friday evening gathering to welcome the Sabbath.
Shul	Synagogue, from the German for school (Yiddish).
Sukkah	A temporary structure, usually with a roof made of branches and leaves, built during the holiday of Sukkot and used for eating meals and sleeping, weather permitting. The sukkah is reminiscent of the huts the Israelites used during 40 years of wandering in the desert.
Shikse	A gentile woman (Yiddish).
Talmud	Rabbinical deliberations concerning Jewish law ethics and customs.
Tefillin	Also known as phylacteries, a pair of black boxes containing biblical verses and worn on the forehead and right arm during morning prayers.
Tallis	Prayer shawl.
Tisha B'av	The ninth day of the month of Av. A day of fasting and mourning the destruction of the first and second temples.
Yeshiva	An institution or rabbinical academy in which Torah, Mishnah and Talmud are taught.
Yiddishkeit	Jewish learning and culture.
Yom Tov	Jewish holiday. A good day (Hebrew).

Introduction

Chienke's Motl and Motl's Chienke is the story of two Jewish human beings, of how destiny, or romance, united them when they were fifteen years old in the year 1925, in the newly organized scout movement, *Hashomer Hatzair,* in Montreal, Quebec, Canada.

They met coincidentally when Motl opened the door for two young girls, fifteen-year-old Chienke and her younger sister, Rochke, who was thirteen. They asked Motl, "Is this where the *Hashomer Hatzair* is?"

"Yes," Motl answered, and the two girls saluted him with the Jewish scout greeting, *"Chazak veamatz!"* (Be strong and be brave).

The girls told him their story. They had arrived a few days earlier from Lithuania, where they already belonged to the *Hashomer Hatzair.* The sweet sixteen party was for a girl who was also a member of the Hashomer, and who had arrived in Montreal from Kishenev, Moldavia, with her mother and two sisters. The party was in their home, in an attic apartment in what was then the poor immigrant district of Montreal.

The two girls were welcomed warmly. The older one, Chienke, had already been the leader of a girl scout group in her Lithuanian town, Pilvishok. She was soon to gain a leading position in the organization in Montreal.

Motl and his parents were Jewish refugees from a small town in the Ukraine. They had been forced to flee in 1920, and were stranded for the next three years in Kishenev, the capital of Moldavia. The American Jewish Joint Relief Committee in Kishenev had established a Hebrew school for the refugee children, one which Motl attended. One of the teachers was named Abraham Shomer. He was a refugee who came from Odessa, in the Ukraine. He felt that the children of the Jewish refugees should be occupied after school to relieve their pain as refugees and to give them an ideal and a goal.

In November, 1923, Motl arrived in Montreal with his parents. Many of the refugee *shomrim*[1] had immigrated to Montreal, Toronto, and Winnipeg with the help of the Canadian Jewish Congress. The Hashomer Hatzair was established on Canadian soil in 1924 by those Jewish refugee children. One of them was Motl.

He was a dreamy youngster who strived stubbornly to become a *chalutz*, a pioneer on a kibbutz in *Eretz Israel*. To accomplish that, he was desperately in need of the warmth and wisdom of Chienke. And from her point of view, Chienke took interest in the stubborn, naive and good-looking dreamer, Motl. This is how the romance started.

In the small towns of Eastern Europe, it was not customary for people to call each other by their family names. If a husband had more prominence and his name was Joseph and his wife's name was Sarah, she was called Joseph's Sarah. If the reverse was true, he was called Sarah's Joseph. As the main personalities in this story have gained equal prominence, their tale is titled, "Chienke's Motl and Motl's Chienke."

Now Motl and Chienke will be separated temporarily to tell their stories, until they reach that point in 1925 when they met in the attic apartment, where the sweet sixteen party was being held. Afterward, from 1925 on, they will tell their life story together, as a gift to their children, grandchildren, nephews, nieces, and great grandchildren, and for the archives of all Jewish public libraries all over the globe. This is the story of Chienke's Motl and Motl's Chienke.

---

[1] Members of the *Hashomer Hatzair*

Chapter 1: Motl's Childhood in the Shtetl of Monastrishch

Part 1: David Darling and Freide

Motl's father, David, was orphaned in childhood. He grew up without a father in a *shtetl* called Monastrishch, in the province of Kiev, in the Ukraine. His education was guided by his mother, Baile, and his Grandfather, Israel Avrum. His mother called him Dovidl Chayesl (David Darling), and that became his nickname in the town.

He was educated first in the traditional *chaider*, then in the *Bet Medrash*, a house of study and prayer, and later in a *Yeshiva*, a seminary in the larger town of Uman. It is there that he became friends with a student named Ali Frumer, who invited him for a Saturday visit to his town, Terniffke. There, David met Freide Frumer, Ali's sister.

Freide was also an orphan, having lost her mother. At eighteen, she was already a *balabusta* (homemaker) and with her good looks she endeared herself to David, who was also eighteen years old. So a few weeks later, he returned with his mother to Terniffke, where their engagement and marriage took place, *bemazal tov.*

Part 2: David and Freide's Family

David and Freide settled in Monastrishch with David's mother. And there, a family with seven children emerged: (from oldest to youngest) Herschel, Sarah, Rochel, Odel, Avrum, Chaike and Motl. Motl was the youngest. *Motl-le*[2] they called him. David established

---

[2] Diminutive form.

himself as one of the most important inhabitants of the town. He was a businessman, with the largest grocery store in the shopping district in the centre of the town.

When the cellar was dug for the construction of their store, evidence of the history of the town was discovered. Caves were discovered beneath the town, and archaeologists claimed they were hideouts for Bogdan Khmelnitsky's Ukrainian gangs, in the Middle Ages. When Motl was a child, he and his older brothers, Hershel and Avrum, went into the cellar with lanterns.

Their father, David, was a thoughtful, well-educated man. A Hasid and a Zionist, he was for many years the director of the synagogue. The mother, Freide, was a helpmate to her husband, a dedicated housekeeper, and was very devoted to her children. There was a saying about her in the town:

> *When David Darling's wife needs milk for her children, and when it happens that there is none, so Freide will issue an order to an empty wall, saying,*
>
> *"Wall, give milk to my children!"*
>
> *And suddenly there will appear a tap and fresh milk will flow to her children.*

Though lacking a formal education, Freide was a talented saleslady in the store. She made a special impression on whomever she met.

Motl's oldest sister, Sarah, grew up as an orderly, well-behaved girl. She helped her mother raise the younger children and was also a good housekeeper. In 1917, just after the communist revolution, she married a veteran of the czarist army, with much music and dancing. During the First World War, he was imprisoned in Hungary, where he became a nurse and druggist. He was also in a gas attack during the war, and was affected by it mentally for the rest of his life. After getting married, they settled in his town, Kenela.

Rochel, the second sister, grew up to be a dynamic girl like her mother. She became a druggist and fell in love with her father's younger cousin. She married him after the big pogrom, without traditional fanfare.

Hershel, the oldest brother, quit school after his bar mitzvah to help in his father's business. But he later changed his mind and decided to become a proletarian and worked in the sugar plant in town.

Odel became a *gymnazistke*, a Russian high school student. She was the oldest of the four younger children and since there was an age gap between them and the three older siblings, these four played and interacted together.

Avrum became "the philosopher," as he was called from the time of his bar mitzvah.

Chaike and Motl, the two youngest in the family, were influenced by the thoughtful *gymnazistke*, Odel, and the dreamer-philosopher Avrum.

Part 3: Motl's Early Childhood

The whole life of the town made a sharp impression on Motl. It was the place in which he spent his early childhood, and it is worthwhile to describe the *shtettele* Monastrishch as he remembered it. It was a Yiddish civilization with a special style of life, a town surrounded by two lakes, connected to the countryside by a bridge and dam on one side, like a peninsula. There was a sugar plant in the town. In the middle of the town there was a main road and a market place surrounded by a few streets where three thousand Jewish inhabitants lived, about five hundred families who created their own world. Gentiles came to the town only to shop for their needs during the week days. They mostly lived in four farm villages on the other side of the river. Aside from trading, there was no interaction between the two communities.

There were six synagogues: the big general *shul*; the *Bet Medrash*, a prayer house and place of voluntary study; the Molotchne *shul*, a prayer house for ordinary people; the Monastrishch Rabbi Court House; a Talner Hassidim prayer house; and a Rachmastrivka Hassidim prayer house, of which Motl's father was the director for many years.

The wealthier families lived in the center of the town, near the sugar plant and the deeper of the two lakes. At the intersection of the lakes, near the Rabbi's court, there lived two wealthy families: the family of Albitier, the owner of a lumber mill, and the family of Maroz, the owner of a leather factory. They were called *appikorsem*, modernized and not very orthodox Jews. The *baale melochos*, or artisans, lived closer to the shallower lake. The *shtetl* was a combination business center and industrial park, which met the needs of the nobility, the farm villagers, and the employees of the sugar plant.

What interested Motl most were the artisans who lived nearby: the blacksmith, the wagon-maker, and the barrel-maker. Motl was very familiar with the bookbinder, who bound books in winter and made cord in summer, as the cord was made outside in front of his house. The cordmaker installed a big wheel. One man wound oakum, which grew near the shallow lake, around his belly and walked backwards for a long distance, producing a thin strand. Entwining many thin strands together produced a special cord used for fetching water from wells.

Next to Motl's house lived the family of Michael Frifeld. He was called Michael, The Ready-Made Clothing-Maker. He manufactured ready-made clothing for the peasantry, in his own house. His store was near Motl's father's store, in the same row. Michael himself used to design and hand-cut the cheap material from the bales of cloth, in the evenings. During the day, he hired Jewish seamstresses who sewed the clothing while singing special Jewish folk songs. The children loved to play around the bales of cloth. Chaike played with the older child, Chana, and Motl with the smaller girl, Sarah, who was nicknamed Sontek. Like a bird, she sang the songs of the seamstresses as well as the Hebrew songs that she had already learned in the Hebrew school.

4

Across from Motl's house lived an old blind man, Yehuda, or Yeudele. When he wanted to go to the synagogue, he needed assistance. So he used to call across from the street, "*Motl-le, vu bist du*" (Motl-le, where are you?). Motl knew already the importance of doing a *mitzvah*. One day, when Motl was leaving his house with a kettle of boiled water to bring to his parents so that they could make tea at their store, he suddenly heard the voice of Yeudele, "*Motl-le, vu bist du?*" Motl had to decide which good deed should come first. So when he saw his girl friend Sontek on her balcony, he pleaded with her, "Take the boiled water to my parents, and I will take Yeude-le to shul, and we will share the mitzvah."

Sontek brought the kettle of boiled water to Motl's parents' store, and she said, "Motl-le led Yeudele to shul, and he asked me to bring the boiled water to you, and he promised to share the mitzvah with me." And she remained standing and waiting. Motl's parents realized that she must not yet understand the real meaning of doing a mitzvah, because she wanted something for it. So they gave her two candies, one for her and one for her friend Motl-le.

The most impressive image of the shtetl in Motl's memory is that of the Sabbath and of holidays. The Sabbath really started on Thursday, when his mother did her shopping and prepared the dough for the *challes* and cookies.

Motl was puzzled on Thursday evenings, when all the women used to disappear. That was the night of the women's ritual bath in the special *mikvah* that adjoined the men's bathhouse that the Germans built when they occupied Ukraine in 1917. The *mikvah* was a big brick building with two huge tanks on the roof, one for cold water and one joined to it with a special wood furnace that made steam for the *shvitz* (steam bath). On Friday afternoon, after a special lunch of stewed meat and Sabbath *challe*, the parade of the males to the bathhouse began: The Zeide, Baruch, Mother's father who visited in the summer, and Father, Hershel, Avrum, and Motl. They sat on the high bench. Motl could not reach high enough to get the steam. He was washed by the elders, and then he played in the men's ritual pool. On leaving the bathhouse, father treated everyone to apple cider. Was it ever good and refreshing!

The girls cleaned and decorated the house for the Sabbath and for holidays. Everyone changed into clean clothing before Friday evening services. They drank tea with Sabbath cookies and then the men paraded to *shul*. Father and Zeide held Motl by the hands while Hershel and Avrum walked behind. People passed by and greeted Zeide, "Good Sabbath, Reb Baruch," and the same to Father, "Good Sabbath, Reb Dovid." Motl asked if they were *rabonim* (rabbis). "Not *rabonim*," father answered, "but that is how well-learned men should be greeted." Still, it was not clear to Motl why his friends' fathers were not addressed as Reb, but instead were just called plain Moishe, Chaim, or Itzik. If not well-learned, they were still good Jews, as good as any others.

On the way back from *shul* it was already dark, and they walked in some fear, until they arrived home, where the lamps were lit and the candles were on the table, with a special tasty Sabbath dinner waiting. There was singing after the meal. The next morning they went to *shul* again. This was followed by a good, pleasant, afternoon rest.

That is how life went on in the kingdom of the small Jewish *shtetl*. The peninsula was all Jewish. The gentile peasantry lived across the lake, and there was no cultural connection between them. Only in trade or business on weekdays did they need to find each other.

Across the lakes, the metallic voices of the young Ukrainians could be heard, sometimes with joy, but also with fear. Yes, a Jewish kingdom was the *shtetl*, surrounded by hostility and fear. But the question is, "Why?" Maybe history will explain it to us. Let us hope for better.

The New Year is supposed to start with the High Holy Days, but in reality, it starts with *Passover*. It is springtime, then, the time for a special cleaning of all homes, the time for buying new clothes for the youngsters, and the special food of the eight days of Passover, with its seder nights and the chanting of the Hagadah, the centuries-old telling of the story of the exodus from Egypt. Then comes *Shavuoth*, the holy day of summertime greenery.

Rosh Hashonah and *Yom Kippur* are the time for taking stock and praying for forgiveness. It was the custom that on the first afternoon of *Rosh Hashonah*, all males and females separated and organized themselves near their synagogues. Saying in unison a special prayer for forgiveness, they marched in parade to the edge of the smaller, shallow lake, where they shook their sins out their pockets into the water of the lake. Chaikele and Motl-le had a wonderful time, then.

In the post-revolutionary year, there was already a secular, cultural life in the town, in which the older youth of the town, including Motl's older sisters and brothers, took part. In addition to a new Hebrew and Yiddish school for children, they organized a public library and a Yiddish theater for amateur artists. The most talented of these was Avadio. He sang and danced and made eyes at the audience—one eye crying and the other eye laughing.

One time, the older children persuaded their mother to attend the theatre. Father would not go. Of course, Mother took the youngest ones, Chaikele and Motl-le, with her. The play was about an orphaned girl. Mother Freide had experienced life as an orphan. She fainted, and Motl-le fell out of her arms.

Despite all these pleasant descriptions of life in the *shtetl*, there were evil things too. There were children of poor Jewish families in the town, and children who grew up without parents to take care of them. They became thieves first, and later, hooligans. And this is the way Motl saw and experienced them.

One Saturday afternoon, Motl and a friend saw three Jewish hoodlums chatting with a domestic girl. At first, she provoked them by flirting. But then the three hoodlums raped her. Motl's friend told him that this is how children are born. The young girl cried and called them, "dirty Jews." Another thing happened with the same hoodlums. It was a summer afternoon. Motl's brother Avrum and his friends took Motl with them for a swim in the bigger lake. The same hooligans brought another beautiful girl with them, and they swam nude with her in front of all the children, until the watchman of the sugar plant came running and yelled at them, "You Goddamned Jews!"

7

Part 4: Pogroms

What Motl remembers first from his childhood is the start of the
First World War in 1914, when he was only four years old. Czarist
soldiers broke into their house, and arrested Father and Hershel on
suspicion that they might be deserters. Mother and *Bubbe* Baile wrung
their hands in fear, but it didn't end badly. They were released because
father was nearsighted and an only son and Hershel, though fully
grown, was only fifteen years old.

Of Kerensky's February revolution in 1917, Motl remembers only
that there was a demonstration in town. None of his family
participated, for fear of what might come out of it. The proletarians
and the assimilated intelligentsia took part in it. Avrum, the
philosopher, fearfully told the children, "Today they holler, 'Down
with the bourgeoisie!' but who knows if later the same people yelling
will shout, 'Down with the Jews!'?"

The Zionist Balfour Declaration was already well known in the
family. Motl's father and the grown-up children were active
organizers in early Zionist gatherings. Motl did not understand a word
of all the speeches that were made. He just held a blue and white flag
and finally fell asleep in his mother's arms.

The period of democratic rule following the Kerensky revolution
was called the "honeymoon months" of Jewish cultural revival in the
shtetl; a time of modern Hebrew education and Zionist and democratic
socialist ideology. The older children registered Chaike and Motl in
the modern Hebrew school without their parents' knowledge. Motl
was taken out of the traditional *cheder*. The new teacher was Pinchas
Tilman, a brother of Sholem Tilman, who had gone to Palestine before
the First World War, during the Ben Gurion era, referred to as the
Second Aliyah.

What remains in Motl's memory of those days is a *Lag b'Omer*
holiday, the one day between *Passover* and *Shavuot* on which
festivities are allowed, when all the children of the *shtetl* were led
singing and dancing by the teachers to a nearby wood. They spent the

whole day playing in the woods, and paraded back to town in the evening.

From all of these happenings, it occurred to little Motle and his friend, Isroleckl, that there was no need to wait; they could travel right then to *Eretz Israel*. They figured out that if they walked along the railroad tracks from the sugar plant, they would reach the nearby railroad station, from which the train would bring them to their objective, Palestine. They began walking along the tracks one hot Saturday morning in the middle of the summer, when a huge rain shower burst out, and the ravine in which the tracks were located was filled with water. Luckily, a farmer drove by and saw the two little boys nearly drowning. He picked them up in his wagon and brought them back that afternoon to Motl's parents' house. They received a spanking, and Motl's first *Aliyah* did not succeed.

The renaissance of the first democratic revolution did not last very long. It was followed by the October communist revolution and, with it, the *pogroms* of the Petlura gangs. One day, the teacher fearfully told the children to run home. The Zeleny gang was on its way to the town, the same gang that had come to the town of Titiev and forced all of the Jews into the biggest synagogue, which they then set on fire. Motl ran home and found that everyone had already left. The fear was so great that everyone had run helter skelter for safety. Motl ran alone on the main road. A friendly gentile recognized him and brought him to his home. Motl shook with fear. The woman of the house realized that he must be hungry, and she gave him a piece of bread spread with lard. It was painful for Motl to eat the non-kosher treat, but his hunger was so great that he did not hesitate. Luckily, the Zeleny gang did not come to Motl's town, but turned instead to another, the town of Sokolivke, which suffered sorely from their villainy.

Eventually, a big pogrom did come to pass in Monastrishch, when Denikin's White Russian army retreated from the Bolsheviks and passed through the town. For three days they massacred, and in a town of only three thousand inhabitants, they killed two hundred and wounded eight hundred, among them Motl's brother, Avrum the philosopher, who was only fifteen years old. He and Motl's grandmother Baile were killed. Rochel's bridegroom Aaron was wounded.

Why only them, when the rest of the family was lucky enough to be saved? Avrum had typhus when this happened. The family, together with over a hundred neighbors, decided to hide out at the little house of Kalmen the shoemaker, which was not very visible from the roadside. It would have been dangerous for the feverish Avrum to travel, and people thought that a regular army would not do bodily harm to a young, sick boy. And to this, the grandmother Baile chimed in and said she would remain to take care of him.

After the three days of that holocaust, they were found dead. The family learned what had happened from a neighbor who was able to see into the house. Avrum, who had a fever, argued and resisted the hooligans. They shot him in the mouth. He used to argue that the Jewish people are like geese. They keep on feeding themselves, while others are being taken out of the next cage to be slaughtered, and they ignore that fact that as soon as they are fattened, they will be slaughtered too. They hacked *Bubbe* Baile with their sabers, while she was pleading with them to have mercy on a young boy who was only fifteen years old.

After the three days of onslaught, it remained for those who were lucky enough to still be alive to do what they could to help the wounded and to bury the dead. A special funeral society (*cheverah kaddisha*) was not yet in existence, so every family had to arrange the funerals of their own dead. Father managed to hire a wagon, and he, Hershel, Odel, and one of Avrum's friends[3] were given the task of gathering the flesh and bones of what remained of *Bubbe* Baile for burial. They ordered their mother, who had fainted when she heard the news, to remain home with the two younger children, Chaike and Motl, but Chaike, the older of the two, could not resist and she ran after the funeral wagon.

---

[3] Hershel Rumick, who in later years became a Yiddish writer.

Motl remained with his mother. When she recovered somewhat, she looked at her hungry Motl-le, and she started thinking about the rest of the family that would return from the cemetery, and about Rochel and her wounded bridegroom. She gained courage and found what food she could in the house, and she cooked a soup to do her best to rescue those who were still living.

Part 5: Planning an Exodus from Russia

Soon after the pogrom, the family started to plan their exodus from the evil country, Russia. The first task was to bring Motl's sister Sarah with her husband, Motl Marianovsky, and their little girl Bella (Buze-le) to their town. First, let the family be together! Then they sent Hershel to sneak across the Romanian border, followed later by sister Rochel and her husband. Then from Kishenev, Romania, they could correspond legally with relatives in Atlanta Georgia, where mother's sister (Dvora) and brother (Joseph)'s families[4] were located. Rochel and her husband would ask them to assist them in their plight. As soon as they were over the border, they sent a note to the rest of the family to follow suit.

The worst incident happened in the summer of 1919, after the pogrom. A self-defense organization had already been organized in the *shtetl*. The Jewish druggist of the town and his family decided to move to Kiev. On the night of their planned departure, it was discovered that they had been robbed and killed. The women were raped first, including the beautiful daughter, Buzy Drapkin. They had tortured her severely. Only one member of the family survived. He had pretended to be dead. In this way he became a living witness who knew who had committed the crime. They were the same Jewish criminals Motl had encountered as a young child.

---

[4] Dvora Samus and Joseph Frumer

How could this have happened with an organized Jewish self defense guard? The guarding was mostly done at the two entrances to the town, one near the bridge connecting the two lakes and the other by the open alleys at the entrance to the peninsula. Nobody could have imagined something like this happening from within.

A common funeral was arranged. Afterward, the criminals were seen sitting on the edge of the bridge, smiling cynically. Not losing the opportunity, the people in the self-defense group apprehended them, not giving them a chance to escape. A special court was elected in the market plaza. They gave them a death sentence, and they were shot on the spot with the slogan, "And you shall erase the evil from within yourselves."

The day of Motl and his family's departure from the town arrived. It was supposed to be kept secret from government officials, but everyone in town knew about it, and on the last day they all came to say farewell to the family of David Darling. Father hired two wagons for the family: Father, Mother, Odel, Chaike and Motl in one; Sarah, her husband[5], and their baby, Buzele, along with the most needed belongings in the other. They hardly slept all night.

Their two best neighbors, Sonteck's father, Michael Frifeld, and Isrolekel's father, Kalmen the shoemaker, walked alongside the wagons for about eight miles. With tears in their eyes, they talked with father; about what, Motl did not know. And so the familiar lifestyle of the *shtetl* was lost to Motl forever and ever.

They drove in the wagons about fifty *versts* (slightly longer than a kilometer) until they came to Motl's mother's town, Ternifke. That night, the family slept at the home of mother's sisters, Aunt Malke Sirkis and Aunt Yeta Gorodetsky. Rifke, Malke's daughter, joined them in their exodus with her husband, Abraham Zaslavsky, a Hebrew teacher from Monastrishch.

---

[5] Motl Marianovsky

Next, they drove on to Bershad, a bigger town, where they saw a Red Army patrol coming toward them. Sarah's husband put on his Red Cross arm band, thinking that they would respect it and not pay attention to them. But the patrol saw this differently. They became suspicious that he might be a Red Army deserter, and they arrested him. Someone was supposed to remain with him, but Sarah had to take care of the baby. Mother was courageous. She went to stay in the city of Bershed until she could obtain his release, using her dynamic personality to plead for his wife and child, and using tears when necessary. It took three weeks.

Meanwhile, the rest of the family had to stay in another town, Chichelnik, in an old fashioned inn. Visitors stayed in the house, and there was a huge shed for the horses and wagons. It was a special occasion for the kids. The young wife of the old owner was a beautiful woman. She was extremely kind to everyone, but she was especially friendly to the children.

When Motl's mother came back with Sarah's husband, they proceeded further on their way. They passed a farm village, and soon noticed that a horse and rider were following them. Eventually, the rider started shooting. The coachman spurred the horses and father ordered them to lie down beneath their effects. The rider followed for some time and then retreated. He did not succeed in robbing them, or maybe doing worse.

They drove on until they came to a wide river, the Bug, which flows into the Black Sea to the South. The only way to cross that river is by a *paron*, a huge wooden raft attached to a cable that is installed on both sides of the river. The cable is pulled so that the raft floats across the width of the river. Motl felt especially good because he also pulled the cable, and that made him feel that he was already grown up.

That same evening, they reached the river Dniester in a town called Rashkov. The other side of the river became Romania, and the townspeople lived on both sides of the river. Because they were divided between two different countries, families were separated. The only thing they could do was to shout to each other across the river. Because they shouted in Yiddish, the border patrols couldn't understand, and in that way it was possible to transmit important messages.

One side of the town was under Soviet rule and there were shortages of everything, while on the other side, in Romania, free enterprise and normal life continued. Motl's family's task was to find a way to smuggle themselves across the Dniester. But how? The smugglers were mostly aligned with the underworld and were not to be trusted.

Father thought up a strategy. They would divide themselves into three groups, so as not to risk all at once. The first group included Father and Mother, Chaike, and Motl. The second group consisted of Sarah with her husband and the baby, with Odel to help take care of the child. The third group included their cousins, Abraham and Rivka Zaslavsky.

Now this is what happened to the first party: As soon as they crossed the river by rowboat, smugglers robbed them of everything and left them wading in water and mud, just as they did with many other people. They waded like that until they reached a wood with some dry ground, where they remained all day until a Romanian shepherd discovered them. He went to his village to inform the villagers of what had happened. The villagers came and arrested them. The village official spoke some Russian, so father, and other elders from a group of stranded people who had crossed earlier, asked him to notify the nearby Jewish village of Verteshen about their plight. Soon, food, dry clothing and other help came to them.

There were already about one hundred people who were prisoners. Motl and the rest of the first group were taken to another, larger, town, Soroca. They had to go through a real trial. They could not say that they had escaped the Petlura gangs and the Czarist armies that the Western countries had sent to fight the Soviet regime. They had to say that they had escaped the torture of the Bolsheviks. By saying this, they were allowed to remain temporarily in Romania as refugees. They did not expect that they would remain there three whole years.

As this happened just before *Passover*, they received a handout of *matzo* from the Joint Distribution Agency (the United Jewish Campaign, in America). A Jewish family invited them for the first days of the holiday. They were well-treated, with much respect given to Father. Rochel joined them from the capitol city of Kishenev, and then their real refugee life started.

It was difficult to find a place to live. They had to rent a *Sukkah* from the family of a widow of a Hassidic rabbi. The widow had a chapel that was in her family's house. It was in a courtyard which was occupied by many neighbors sharing common toilet facilities, consisting of four square sheds with no plumbing.

Next to them there lived a couple, a dealer of second-hand clothing, a bitter man. But his wife, Mommtzie, was a good soul. If not for her, they would have frozen when Fall started. She used to take them into her house, which had an oven.

In Moldavia there is plentiful fresh fruit and vegetables in summer. Mother Freide's courageous nature also helped them to survive. She bought a couple of chickens. She raised them and they laid eggs, so that she could give one egg each to Chaikele and Motl-le.

The Joint Distribution Agency organized afternoon Hebrew schools. They could not get new school buildings, so they used a school building after regular school days. That meant that the refugee children would have school hours from three in the afternoon. The teaching staff was recruited from the refugee intelligentsia, of whom there were many. One of them was Abraham Shomer. He organized the kids into the *Hashomer Hatzair*, a Hebrew Scouts organization.

Chaike was then thirteen years of age, so she joined the real scouts, in which there were boys and girls together. Motl was eleven, so he joined a young boy's group called the Pioneers. This was an important milestone in the lives of the two youngest children of the family. Chaike was more dynamic, like their mother. Motl was more dreamy and considerate, like their father. Chaike always had a grievance that she was punished mostly because of her little brother Motl-le. When she went on a hike, Motl-le wanted to go with her. More than once she was punished for taking along her dreamy little brother. This was in her character until her last days.

Motl took the idea of being a *shomer* very seriously. A *shomer* has to be kind to people and to animals. He must perform at least one good deed every day. For this, Motl woke up early in the morning to help his mother carry the shopping bag.

One day, Mother wanted to buy Motl-le a treat to eat, but Motl had to refuse. Why? Because to build strong character, he and his friends had made a pledge not eat special foods for a month, but to eat only to exist. When Motl told this to his mother, she still could not understand. If one does not eat better food will it make him a better person? Motl had to explain to her that the Jewish people must stop coddling themselves. Otherwise they will forever remain in exile in the *galut*. Mother loved to tell that story all her life, even when her son Motl-le had himself become a father and even a grandfather.

To survive in Kishenev during those three years, Father became a secretary to a Hassidic rabbi. That was a brief but comfortable time, during which the children enjoyed better food from the *rebbe*'s leftovers.

Hershel began sending them five dollars a month as soon as he arrived in Canada. Why Canada? Because the quota for entering the United States was filled. To enter Canada, one only had to prove that he possessed $250. So their relatives in Atlanta sent the money and first Hershel and later, in 1921, Rochel and her husband went to Montreal.

In Kishenev, Odel worked in a factory making wooden heels for women's shoes. Motl's mother, tried to start a little business with a fruit stand in the market, but this was illegal. When a Romanian policeman asked to see her permit and found that she had none, he became vicious and threw all the fruit to the ground. This frightened her terribly and she became very ill.

For two years, the children, Chaike and Motl, enjoyed the Hebrew school and the *Hashomer*. When Motl turned twelve and was soon to be bar-mitzvahed, his father felt that he could no longer keep him in a secular school, and he enrolled him in the Kishenev *yeshiva*. Motl was sad to separate from Jewish secular ideology. That was the first thing that changed Motl and Chaike's childhood friendship. Later in life, Motl appreciated his short experience as a yeshiva student. It made him more knowledgeable about traditional *Yiddishkeit*.

After three years, the Romanian government became fed up with the Jewish refugees from Russia.They gave them an ultimatum: Emigrate or be expelled back to Soviet Russia. Father alerted the children in Canada, asking them to find someone to bring Odel and Chaike, who was already fifteen years old, to Canada as domestics. And they did. Hershel would be able to get an entry permit for his father and mother and the twelve-year-old minor, Motl. But as soon as Odel and Chaike left, the Romanian authorities became apprehensive about the refugees being near the Soviet border, so they banished all of them to the capitol city of Bucharest for a while. Father, Mother, and Motl had to experience *galut* again in Bucharest for three months, and Sarah and her family for a year more.

The order came on the day of Yom Kippur, 1923. They were loaded like sheep into freight wagons in special trains and all in one day taken to Bucharest. They were stationed in old army barracks near the Jewish neighborhood. Whole families had to sleep together like sheep on wooden bunks. All had to cook and eat in the same place, if they had anything to eat.

No one could bear the rivalries between families, so Father decided to try to rent some private space. He, Sarah's husband and Motl went out to look for a place. They saw a sign "Room for Rent," so they went in and found an extremely religious woman with a wig on her head. A girl lay in bed reading a bible in the other room. The woman said it was her daughter and that she was sick. But when they went out into the street, neighbors told Father a secret about what was really going on there: The woman ran a brothel and the sign was only for the purpose of attracting men. So they gave up the idea of renting a private living space.

Part 6: Canada

In November, 1923, Father, Mother and Motl got visas for Canada, and finally left Bucharest by train, traveling through Hungary and Czechoslovakia and then through Germany. Hitler's first coup attempt was that year, and all was in chaos. They had to change trains. At one point Motl was separated from his parents and they lost each other. Luckily, they found themselves together at a station. In Hamburg, they had to pass a quarantine test. At last they boarded a small ship to Southampton and then a larger ship, *The New Zealand*, to Halifax.

Father and Mother suffered sea sickness, but not Motl. He helped his parents and others. On the trip by train from Halifax, Motl observed the Eastern Canadian landscape. Canada was a large country. But how would they settle there in the near future?

Motl's brother Hershel met them at the train station in Montreal, and they arrived at the home of Rochel and Aaron (Arke) Lerman, a second floor flat in a wooden house that consisted of four small rooms in the Jewish district around the main street, St. Lawrence, with Mount Royal visible nearby. The house had toilet facilities, but no bath. They had to use the public bath in the neighborhood.

Motl walked the streets in the fall, with winter looming. Montreal was a big city. There was no comparison with Motl's hometown in the Ukraine and with Kishenev, in Southern Moldavia. A *landsman* came and took Motl to register in the English public school. Because he didn't understand English, Motl had to start from the beginning with the nine-year-old kids, although he was already thirteen years old. The teachers promised that if he learned quickly, they would let him skip classes, and that is how it was. The teacher, Miss Smith, asked Motl to remain after school to tutor him, so he finished elementary school at the age of fifteen.

The same *landsman* also took Motl to register in the Jewish People's School. It was on the same street as the other school. A good-looking man of twenty-five examined Motl in *Yiddishkeit*. Motl was assigned to a secondary school and later to a higher level, with youngsters his own age and even older.

Motl made friends with some of the students and started to agitate for *chalutziut*[6] among them. One friend, Pinchas, had come to Canada with his mother to join his father, who had come before World War I. He had finished high school at the age of sixteen and had already entered McGill University.

In the mid 1920s, Palestine was in crisis. So Pinchas came up with an idea: "We should first acquire homestead land from the Canadian government, so that we can gain experience and preparation in farming." Pinchas was the kind of person who speaks and then acts right away. Within weeks, they received an acceptance letter with full plans for a collective settlement. As it turned out, the plans remained just plans.

They could not all live in Rochel's small house, so they rented a house on a nearby street. They had to move in through the snowy winter streets. The children were happy. Hershel and Odel gladly painted and decorated the new home. But there was a problem as to how their father could earn a living. Although he was then only fifty years old, the same age as their mother, he could not work in a factory in his Hassidic clothing. Also, with her dynamic character, Mother needed something to occupy herself.

Another *landsman* gave them a suggestion. The landlord from whom the house was rented was a coal delivery-man, and he wanted to earn extra income. So he had opened a store downstairs from the rented house. He tried to get his wife to run it but that didn't work out. The *landsman* said, "David and Freide, you take over the store. You will make a go of it." And that is how it was.

During their first two years in Canada, most of the Jewish refugees from Romania came to Canada with the help of the Canadian Jewish Congress. Among them were Motl's sister, Sarah, with her husband, Motl Marianovsky, and baby, Buzele. Thus, the whole family was

---

[6] Zionist pioneering

reunited. But a new problem arose with Motl Marianovsky. He could not be a nurse or even a druggist in Canada, and he refused to do other work. A brother of his, who lived in Buffalo, New York brought him over there and thus relieved the family of that issue.

These immigrants included more members of the *Hashomer Hatzair* movement, some of whom were older. With their encouragement, Chaike and Motl decided to organize the *Hashomer Hatzair of Canada*, with the help of Zionists in Montreal, who allowed them to use a basement for gatherings. The same thing happened in Toronto and Winnipeg. Later, new *shomrim* began to arrive from Poland and Lithuania, and they gladly joined too.

And with that, we come to the sweet sixteen birthday party, where Motl and Chienke met for the first time and where the romance, *Chienke's Motl and Motl's Chienke*, began.

Jacob's Commentary

My father grew up in the Ukraine, in a village located not far from its capital city of Kiev. Ukraine, the southwestern region of the former Soviet Union, is today an independent state and has been so since the demise of the Soviet Union toward the end of the 20th century. However, for much of the last few hundred years of European history this area was under Russian or Soviet domination. In fact, Ukraine was a major component of the so-called Pale of Settlement, the region in which Jews of the Russian Empire were permitted to inhabit. This policy was intended to keep Jews out of the Russian heartland; that is, Moscow and St. Petersburg. Along with other areas of the Pale, such as White Russia (Belarus) and Lithuania, the Ukraine included a large Jewish population of about 5 million. In 1900, this number represented almost half of the estimated total world Jewish population of 11 million. Today, the numbers are far smaller, as a result of large waves of emigration in the early and late portions of the 20th century (to the United States in the early years of the century, and largely to Israel during the last period of the century). Of course the numbers are also smaller as a result of the Holocaust. An estimate of the Jewish population of Ukraine in 2000 placed the number at less than 200,000.

There has been some speculation as to how such large numbers of Jews ended up inhabiting this area of Eastern Europe. One of the more controversial theories involves the story of the Khazars, a semi-nomadic tribe of Turkic people that inhabited a large area north of the Caucasus mountains, between the Caspian Sea and the Black Sea[7]. An independent and influencial Khazar state existed from about the seventh century until the tenth century, when it was overrun by external, mainly Russian, forces. Of interest to Jews is the fact that Judaism became the state religion of Khazaria from the eighth or ninth century. Why this occurred is not known, although one suggestion indicates that it was part of an effort to remain neutral in response to pressures from the Christian world and the Moslem world that surrounded this area. Judaism, as precursor to both Islam and Christianity, may have been considered an acceptable alternative. Some suggest that it was only the nobility and the leadership that actually converted to Judaism while other archeological evidence suggests that conversion was widespread among the general population as well.

Whatever the reason for the Khazar conversion to Judaism, this episode has held a fascination for many Jews, including myself. I first learned about the Khazars as a student in the Jewish parochial school I attended, probably when I was in the eighth or ninth grade. My class was exposed to the work of the famous twelfth-century Spanish Jewish poet, Rabbi Yehuda Halevi. The work, titled *Kuzari*, is presented as a dialog between the pagan king of the Khazars and a Jewish scholar who was teaching him the fundamentals about Judaism.

---

[7] From Wikipedia

My interpretation of the fascination surrounding this story is simply that in comparison to the long and often tragic narrative of the history of the Jewish people, here was a romantic and epic tale about an independent and strong Jewish state that, for a while, played an important role in world events. In recent years I also read a book by Arthur Koestler titled, *The Thirteenth Tribe*. Published in 1976, the book proposes that the Jews of Eastern Europe are or were the descendents of the Khazars. Genetic research has debunked this idea, in that both European Jews (*Ashkenazi*, from the Hebrew for "Germany") and non-European Jews (*Sephardi* from the Hebrew for "Spain") are genetically linked to each other and to Middle Eastern groups such as the Palestinians. Nevertheless, this hasn't stopped anti-Semites and anti-Zionists from jumping on this point as a means of denying the Jewish claim to a homeland in Palestine.

My father brings up two Ukrainian historical figures, namely Bogdan Khmelnitsky and Symen Petlura. Khmelnitsky was a Cossack leader (*hetman*) from Ukraine who led a popular uprising to create an independent Ukrainian state from 1648 to 1654. At that time, Ukraine was dominated by the rulers of the powerful Polish-Lithuanian regime that dominated much of Central/Eastern Europe. While Khmelnitsky is considered a national hero in Ukraine today, his memory is an abomination as far as Jews are concerned. Basically, the Jews, who often acted as an interface between the ruling elite and the peasants, were primary targets of the roaming Cossack bands and estimates of the number of Jews massacred during this period range as high as 500,000. In spite of occasional episodes of resistance, usually behind the ramparts of fortress synagogues, it has been estimated that as many as 700 Jewish communities were devastated during this period. In fact, this event was considered to be the most tragic event in Jewish history before the Holocaust. The meteoric rise of the most famous of the false Jewish messiahs, Sabbatai Zevi, shortly after the Khmelnitsky massacres, is attributed to the despair that characterized Jewish feeling at that time.

Petlura was a more modern Ukrainian hero who led the fight for the establishment of an independent Ukraine in the period after the Russian Revolution. He was briefly (1919-1920) the head of a Ukrainian state. However, as in the case of Khmelnitsky, Petlura is also remembered as being at least in part responsible for the terrible anti-Jewish pogroms that accompanied the Russian Civil War that broke out in the years after the Russian Revolution. It has been estimated that between 70,000 and 250,000 Jews were killed in Russia during this time by the various combatants, including the White Russian forces, the Bolsheviks, and the forces under Petlura. Petlura's effort failed in the end, and he escaped to Paris, where he was assassinated by a Jew from Ukraine, in 1926. Today, Petlura is considered a Ukrainian hero, the toast of special events that are celebrated in his memory and the subject of a number of monuments. However, in Jewish history he represents a dark chapter, once again only eclipsed by the terrible events that were to follow, the Holocaust.

My father's mention, in this chapter, of my grandfather's belonging to a specific Hassidic group was the first indication I had that there was a Hassidic family connection. My grandfather died when I was in elementary school, but I remember him well. He wore the garb of a typical orthodox East European Jew, including a black skullcap and a black kaftan, and he had a large gray beard. However, it never occurred to me that he would have been a Hasid or that he belonged to a specific group. From a recent reading of *Boychiks in the Hood: Travels in the Hasidic Underground*, by Robert Eisenberg, a popular book describing the variety of Hassidic activity in North America and elsewhere, I first became aware of the existence of the large number and variety of Hasidic sects. Media attention has focused on the Chabad Lubavitch Hassidim because of their extensive public outreach activities and the former charismatic Rebbe Schneerson, who passed away in 1994. I was also aware of the Satmer Hassidim because of their large numbers and anti Zionist views. Recent news items in sources such as the Jerusalem Report have reported on the devotees of Rabbi Nachman of Breslov, whose memory draws about 20,000 Hasidic pilgrims to the Ukraine every Rosh Hashanah

The Rachmastrivka dynasty is named after a town in the Ukraine. The dynasty was founded by Rabbi Yochanan Twersky the son of one of the disciples of the Baal Shem Tov ("Master of the Good Name"), the founder of Hasidism. It is an offshoot of an earlier dynasty founded in Chernobyl, and it still exists. It is considered to be one of the larger Hasidic groups[8]. There are two Rebbes, one in Brooklyn and the other in Jerusalem.

My grandfather was a sensitive man. One of my father's favorite stories was about an episode that took place in Bucharest when his parents were applying for Canadian visas. The Canadian consul, who was a Jewish man, accused my grandfather of lying in his deposition with respect to the various family members' ages. There may in fact have been some bending of the truth in order to fit appropriate immigration categories. My grandfather, who may or may not have known the details, was devastated by the accusation and went home to be bedridden for some time. It was left to Motl and his mother to plead for understanding from the consul, until the proper visas were granted.

From my father's comments, I have been under the impression that my father's family would have actually preferred to immigrate to the United States, where some distant relatives already resided. Jewish immigration to the United States was more or less unrestricted between the last years of the nineteenth century until about 1921, and about two million Jewish immigrants entered the country during that time period. However, restrictions on immigration, including the 1921 Johnson Emergency Quota Act and the Immigration Act of 1924, removed that possibility. The restrictions were based on early and erroneous measures of intelligence indicating that Southern and Eastern Europeans and Jews were intellectually deficient, a point discussed by Stephen Jay Gould in *The Mismeasure of Man* (1981). Immigration to Canada was equally restrictive; between 1921 and 1931 only about 16,000 Jews were admitted to Canada. However, after the establishment of the US quota on immigration, Canadian restrictions were comparatively relaxed for a brief period, and this must have been the reason for my father's family's success in their efforts to become Canadians. Likely, the same set of circumstances affected my mother's family, with the result that they too immigrated to Canada at about the same time. In fact, during the 1930s and

---

[8] Wikipedia

through the period of World War II, Canadian immigration policy became very restricted as far as Jews were concerned, partly due to the widespread economic depression, but also due to anti-semitism. As Irving Abella and Harold Troper documented in the book, *None is Too Many,* "Canada's record in saving Jews from the Holocaust was the worst of virtually any other country in the world". While I have felt very comfortable as a Canadian in general, this fact, the inaction and, even worse, the active anti-Jewish behavior of Canadian officialdom at a time of greatest Jewish need, continues to give me pause from time to time as I go about my daily life.

Chapter 2: Mary and Gershon's Chienke

Part 1: Life in Pilvishok

Chienke was born in a small Lithuanian *shtetl* called Pilvishok, in Yiddish (Pilviskiai, in Lithuanian), then a part of Russia. She was the eighth surviving child, the fifth girl, of the family. Her father, Gershon, a scholar and businessman, was a veteran of the Czarist army. It was said that he continued to observe morning Jewish prayers, while wearing *tfillin* on his head and a *tallis* around his shoulders, even when he was on guard duty. When another soldier reported him to the officer, saying; "What a funny soldier, how can we depend on him to stand guard?" The officer replied, "People of faith, even Jewish ones, are the most dependable soldiers."

Chienke's mother, Mary Gershon's, as she was called, was a sympathetic woman with a fine sense of humour that helped her in her lifelong struggle. Chienke's oldest brother, Hirshel, helped his father while still a child, because he had caught chronic bronchitis during his service in the Czar's army. The smaller children called Hirshel "Little Father." Hirshel always brought goodies for the children when he returned from a business trip. One time he knocked on the window late at night to waken Chienke and her mother. Hirshel had to tell her that this time he didn't have presents. Chienke, a child only four years old, said, "But Hirshel, I love you just the same."

When the time came for Hirshel to serve in the Czar's army, Mary wanted to send him to her brother in America, but Father couldn't send his eldest son away when his help was needed at home. He thought Hirshel should serve his three years, and he did. Hirshel became a soldier in 1913, one year before the start of the First World War. In 1914 Hirshel was among the first echelons to go to the battlefield. Mary and her children stood by the highway as the soldiers marched through town on their way to the front. They looked for Hirshel in order to give him some good things to eat. As they didn't see him, the goodies were handed over to the other soldiers.

Chienke's father's sickness became more serious. He also felt guilty for not having allowed his son to leave for America. Leah, the oldest sister, was a scholarly individual with a knowledge of languages. Since the town's only doctor had left, she convinced an army doctor to examine Father. The doctor concluded that nothing could help their father. One of his lungs had been removed in earlier years and now the second one was failing.

Mary and her daughters attended Chienke's father at his bedside. When Chienke fell off a chair and hurt her head, her mother fainted. Father said, "Mary, you must have courage. You cannot afford to faint in these circumstances." He meant to say after his death. This was his last concern.

Some of the children ran to the *Bet Medresh*[9] to ask for prayers of mercy to be said for their father. Their brother Itzel was traveling to the capital city of Kovno (Kaunas) to bring needed produce back to town. At night, he dreamt that father was lying on the floor with lit candles near his head. He rushed back to town to see his mother and the three smallest children, Rivke, Chienke and Rochele standing near his dying father. When their mother cried out, "Gershon, who will I and the children depend on now?" their father raised his hands and said "On the mercy of God."

Chienke's father died on the eighteenth day of Shevat, 1915. During the days of mourning, mother gained strength. She began to prepare meals for her family with whatever food she could find. Chienke noticed that her mother cut a herring into eight pieces, one for each of the children. She pleaded with her mother to cut the fish into nine pieces.

Meanwhile, the war continued. The German army occupied the town and sent all produce to Germany. Chienke's family earned a living by baking pastry for the Germans in the large family oven. The

---

[9] Study house

28

two younger brothers, Itzel and Oishel (Harry), who were 18 and 13 years old, smuggled horses and cows across the river for a Jewish merchant. Both boys were strong swimmers and the river near town was an administrative border imposed by the Germans. One time the brothers were caught and arrested. They didn't reveal the name of the person they were smuggling for. When the town's Rabbi asked mother to tell the boys to tell the Germans what they wanted to know, she refused. She would never tell her sons to be informers. In any case, the brothers were released because they were minors. Mother would not let them smuggle again. Instead, the family turned to the production of soap from the fats of the hindquarters of slaughtered cows. Two of the sisters, Raizel and Sorke, were given the job of getting the soap across the border to Vilna, the capital city. This they did by wrapping the soap around their bodies and then covering it with large coats. After the Purim holiday, the family was given the concession to bake Passover matza for the town.

The war went on. At first the Germans were victorious. They established a one-room school, and attendance was compulsory. The teacher was a German Jew who had been wounded at the front, and Chienke was one of his favorite pupils. Because of her knowledge of German, many of the townspeople, both Jews and Lithuanians, came to Leah for assistance in filling out documents and writing letters. She was also employed as a Hebrew teacher. This provided some additional income for the family. The family celebrated when a letter came through the Spanish consulate to let them know that Hirshel was alive and well and in a prisoner of war camp in Austria.

At this point, an offensive by the Russian army led to a German retreat. The Germans announced that the town would be put to the torch. The inhabitants had no choice but to cross the river to get away from the expected inferno. This was no easy task, for the bridge had been destroyed. Chienke's family managed to get across, although a *zaide* and a *bubbe* as well as an elderly aunt were left behind. They were on the other side of the river. Mother remarked that she hoped that the *zaide* and *bubbe* would open the door of the stable so that the horse and the cow could escape. Then Oishel reminded her that he had the only key to the stable. So Oishel ran back to the town, unlocked the animals, and took them along with the rest of the family to the village on the other side of the river.

Life was hard. They slept on the floor of a shack that they rented from a peasant. Somehow, with the help of milk from their cow, mother managed to feed the whole family, as well as a few of the neighbors who were in even worse circumstances.

At the end of that summer the war came to an end and Lithuania became an independent state. The family returned to their burned-out home. With the help of a hired hand, Antanis, they managed to sow and reap enough potatoes to survive and reestablish their home. Their surprise and joy was great when Hirshel came home!

Hirshel was not the same person he was before the war. His voice was different and he was saddened to learn of his father's passing. Hirshel vowed to reestablish himself and to assume responsibility for the family. But Mother wouldn't hear of such a thing. Before the war, Hirshel had been romantically involved with a cousin from the nearby city of Mariampol. The cousin had waited for Hirshel throughout the war. Over Chienke's objections (she didn't want to lose her little father again) Mother convinced Hirshel to get married.

Life in Lithuania went back to normal, and Jews were given a degree of cultural autonomy. Although it lacked textbooks, a Hebrew school was established. The teachers translated on the blackboard from other languages. Primitive as the facilities were, the level of instruction was very high. Leah became one of the teachers. This made it difficult for Chienke, the student, since any problem would be immediately reported to Mother. But it didn't matter since Mother always took Chienke's side.

Instruction in the Lithuanian language was compulsory in the schools. Since the Lithuanian teacher was an ineffective drunkard, the government recruited Jewish students and sent them to Kaunas (Kovno), the capital, for language training in Lithuanian. Aside from the study of Lithuanian, all subjects were taught in Hebrew, in the more modern Hebrew schools. The teachers and students were attracted to the ideals of such Zionist movements as *Hatchia*,

Hechalutz, Hatzair and *Hashomer Hatzair*. Chienke, and later Rochke, became involved with other girls and boys in a group of young Jewish scouts. There were summer excursions to the nearby woods and towns to meet and discuss various aspects of pioneering life in Palestine. Chienke began as a drummer girl and later became a leader of her group.

At this time Chienke's mother began to correspond with her brothers in the United States. In addition to providing financial help, they planned to bring the family to America. Itzel and Oishel would be brought over first, before they were drafted into the Lithuanian army. However, the introduction of a quota system for immigration to the United States meant that this door was now closed. Instead, mother's brothers contacted their father's brother in Montreal, Canada. They sent him money to help arrange Itzel and Oishel's immigration to Montreal.

The departure of two of her sons was difficult for mother, but she persevered. For years later, Chienke remembered how her mother celebrated the start of the Sabbath on Friday evenings by lighting the Sabbath candles with all six girls. She would say the *Kiddush* and they would sing Sabbath hymns (*zmirot*). Meanwhile, Chienke's two brothers in Montreal began to send money to Mother while planning how to bring the rest of the family to Canada. The initial plan was for the two older sisters, Leah and Raizel, to immigrate first, but Leah refused in favour of Raizel's fiancé, Meir. Leah also felt that she should remain with her mother and younger sisters, as she was the family's only provider. And that is what happened. Raizel and Meir were married in Mariampol, the city Hirshel lived in, and then left for Canada. Leah remained in Pilvishok for the time being and became a celebrated Hebrew teacher.

Due to the influence of idealistic Zionist teachers such as their sister Leah, Chienke and Rochke were well versed in Hebrew. The training they received in the *Hashomer Hatzair* prepared them for a pioneering life in Palestine. However, life takes its own course. With brothers Itzel and Oishel already in Canada, along with Raizel and Meir Coviensky, an effort was made to bring the rest of family too. First, it was arranged that Leah would immigrate as a domestic.

However, when Leah visited the Canadian consul in Riga (Latvia) in order to obtain a visa, the consul, looking at her hands and face, decided that she was too delicate to work as a housemaid. New papers arrived from Canada showing that Leah was needed as a teacher in a Hebrew School. This time she had no trouble getting her visa from the same consul.

Now it was the rest of the family's turn. But there were problems. Mother's health was deteriorating, while Sorke had a boyfriend, Yosel, whom she didn't want to leave behind. Rivke was deeply involved in the *Hashomer Hazair* movement. She had to be convinced to stick with the family and continue to prepare for the kibbutz way of life from Canada.

Meanwhile, life in Pilvishok continued. A group of young men, all in the *chalutz* movement, arrived in town from Poland. The young men were trying to avoid military service in the Polish army while at the same time getting work experience that would be useful for their future *aliyah* to Palestine. The young men worked hard for poor wages. To save money, and because they were not very observant, they bought non-kosher meat. Once, when they were visiting, Mother asked how they cooked their meat. They said that they had a problem in that they lacked a large pot. Mother felt sorry for them. She asked Chienke to get the large copper Passover pot from the attic. To Chienke's inquiring look Mother said, "We are going away to Canada anyway, and if we ever need the pot again we can re-kosher it." A few days later the rabbi complained to Mother about the *chalutzim* buying non-kosher meat. He threatened to excommunicate them and report them to the authorities for entering Lithuania illegally. Mother became angry and admitted to lending them her pot. She turned to her children and said, "Look at that. When these young men were freezing for lack of fuel during the winter and starving for lack of food nobody cared. And now our rabbi wants to turn them over to the police!"

Mary and her daughters received the proper documents to enable them to immigrate to Canada, but then Mary became very ill. This was difficult for the girls to accept. After all, their mother was only fifty years old. When her condition became critical they became very worried and sent a message to Hirshel. He came, and when she noticed that he was well-dressed, wearing new yellow shoes, she said that she was sorry that didn't have four more sons with yellow shoes instead of the four daughters she was leaving with yellow faces. Those were her last words. Hirshel and the four girls cried but their mother was no longer alive. Hershel's family, along with the chief rabbi of Mariampol, arrived for the funeral. The four girls insisted that that the eulogy be said by the rabbi of their town since he had known their mother so well.

During *shiva*, the mourning period, Hirshel made plans to bring his four youngest sisters back to Mariampol to live with him. But the sisters, led by Sorke, decided to stay in their town until new papers arrived allowing them to immigrate to Canada without their mother. When they finally went to Riga to get their visas the consul rejected Rochke because she limped from a bout with polio. Although Hirshel offered to take Rochke in to live with his family, the girls refused to leave without her. They returned to Pilvishok where they renewed their various social activities. Chienke and Rochke were active once more in *Hashomer Hatzair*.

Part 2: Immigration to Canada

Eventually, new papers arrived. This time a prominent businessman guaranteed to be responsible for Rochke's upkeep. But in the papers her name had been changed to Minnie. Once again the four sisters travelled to Riga to see the Canadian Consul. Rivke, always the pessimist, kept reminding Rochke to answer to the name of Minnie when she was before the consul. But when the consul called for Minnie, Rivke forgot herself and said, "Rochke, they're calling you."

This time they got their visas. Their friends arranged a farewell party for them. They promised to meet each other again in Palestine. The sisters went from house to house to say good-bye to neighbors and relatives. In spite of the many hardships they had experienced, leaving home was painful. Chienke, a fifteen-year-old girl with her own thoughts and ideals about an enlightened Jewish way of life, wondered what they would find in the new world.

The sisters travelled overland to Hamburg, Germany. Their brother, Hirshel, and Sorke's boyfriend, Yosel, accompanied them to the German border. In Hamburg they spent some time in quarantine. There, they met many immigrants who were stranded because of legal problems. Although the sisters had their visas, Rivke worried that they too might become stranded. She cautioned the others against giving away any of their food or belongings - just in case. Nevertheless, they passed the various examinations and formalities and boarded the ship that would take them to Canada.

On board, Chienke didn't feel well. She missed her friends and her brother Hirshel. He had truly been like a father to her. They met Canadian children returning from visits to relatives in Europe. To Chienke, the Canadian youngsters appeared to act childishly. When she was given her first banana, she found it to be tasteless and threw it overboard while the Canadian children laughed.

When the ship finally arrived at Quebec City, they telephoned Raizel in Montreal to let her know that they had arrived. The four sisters arrived in Montreal by train at the time of Succot in the year 1925.

The two older sisters, Leah and Raizel, did their best to make a home for their younger sisters. At first they lived with Raizel and her husband Meyer (whom they knew from home) and their two little boys, Gershon and Moishe. Leah, who married another Meyer, lived next door with their brothers, Oishel and Itzel. The brothers helped their newly-arrived sisters buy Canadian-style clothing, while Leah registered the younger sisters, Chienke and Rochke, in elementary school.

Chienke and Rochke felt out of place in school because they were placed into grades with younger children. They were happy to skip classes one day when they were invited to a sweet sixteen party. And here we come to the party where Chienke met Motl. From this point onwards their stories will be told together.

Jacob's Commentary

My knowledge of my mother's early life stems from a mixture of stories she told to me when I was a child. The major event in her early years concerned the effect that World War I had on her small community in Lithuania. Before the war, Lithuania was a part of greater Russia. Various nationalist organizations agitated for independence and a return to the former glories of the of the Polish-Lithuanian bi-national state that existed in the sixteenth and seventeenth centuries. The most recent episode was an uprising that took place in 1905, the same year as the failed Russian revolution. During the First World War, Russia, an ally of the French, the British and the Italians, faced the Central powers, consisting of the Austro-Hungarian Empire and Germany. While the Russian army was successful initially in facing the Austro-Hungarian forces, the large, poorly equipped and ineptly-led Russian army was no match against the Germans. By the summer of 1915, a little less than one year after the start of the war, Lithuania had been over-run by the German army. The Germans remained in control of Lithuania for most of the three-year period, until the end of the war and the capitulation of Germany in November 1918. As a result, my mother's first years of general schooling were in German and she retained an ability to speak German throughout her life. I can still recall the words and tune to the German anthem, "Deutschland Uber Alles" and the popular Christmas song "Tanenbaum" from hearing them sung by my mother. I can also recall an antisemetic ditty that she sang although I don't know where she heard it. It goes as follows: "Die mutter kocht nudels, die vater mischsed aus, dhen kammen zwei yuden und fressen es aus" (mother cooks noodles, father stirs them, then two Jews come and gobble them up).

The Jewish community in Lithuania, which was fairly large, about 100,000 in 1918, was well-organized. It was a major centre of Jewish scholarship and a rival to the Hasidic movement, which was fundamentalist in nature and located mainly in Polish cities and towns. In fact, Vilnius (known in Yiddish as Vilna), the ancient capital of the Kingdom of Poland-Lithuania, was known as the "Northern Jerusalem."

Ownership of Vilnius was a point of contention between Poland and Lithuania after they both regained their independence following World War I. Vilnius actually became a part of Poland during the inter-war period and did not become the capital of Lithuania until after World War II. In my mother's time, the lesser city of Kovno (Kaunus) was the capital city.

As was true for most of the Jewish population of Eastern Europe, the Jews of Lithuania spoke Yiddish in everyday life. I don't think that the origins of Yiddish are very clear, but since Yiddish consists mainly (about 80%) of German words (albeit written with the Hebrew alphabet) it must have originated in a more central or western portion of the European continent. As a result, the Jews of Lithuania could interact with the German soldiers and administrators that inhabited their region of Europe during the three years of German occupation. My mother began elementary school during this period. The times were difficult, as in any wartime situation, but my mother never indicated that the Jews were dealt with more harshly than the rest of the population. I do recall her stories about the burning of Pilvishok and how her family had to flee across a damaged railroad bridge to escape the inferno. I think the wooden ties that bind the rails were broken or burned and that crossing over meant walking along the narrow rails. This was something her mother Mary could not do until finally a stranger offered to carry her across. The family had a difficult time, surviving the winter in some form of outbuilding, or shack. But at least they had a milk cow, saved by my uncle Oishel, and the cow helped them survive by providing milk for the family in addition to being a commodity that could be bartered for other needs.

As is true of most children, I wasn't that concerned with my mother's early life when I was younger. Now that I am interested, she's not around to fill in the gaps. So I don't know the dates associated with the burning of the town of Pilvishok. It may have happened more than once as armies moved to and fro across the landscape, as she indicated in the earlier part of this chapter. It may have happened during the turbulent time after the war, roughly between 1918 and 1922, when various factions and militias fought each other during a time referred to as the Russian Civil War. The factions would have included the Bolsheviks, fighting to maintain what was a tenuous grip on what was the former Russian Empire, right-wing Russian groups fighting to defeat the Bolsheviks and sponsored in part by anti-Bolshevik elements from the western powers, as well as various nationalist factions fighting to regain the independence of the Baltic States (including Lithuania), as well as Polish forces fighting for Polish independence. At the end of it, Poland and Lithuania did achieve independence, although the prized city of Vilnius became a part of Poland.

Lithuanian independence lasted from about 1922 until 1940, when the country was overrun by the USSR as a part of the pact between Stalin and Hitler, which also led to the partitioning of Poland. Russian dominance, however, was short-lived as the country was again over-run by the Germans after the German attack on the USSR in 1941. This time, a mere twenty-odd years after the last German occupation, the experience of the Jewish population was very different. Over ninety percent of Lithuanian Jewry was murdered by Germans, actively assisted by the Lithuanian population. In fact, one of the most disturbing episodes that I have ever read concerning the Holocaust, and I have read a lot, was a description of the brutality by the general population of Lithuania towards their Jewish neighbors during the initial German takeover of the country. My mother's elder brother, Hirshel, his wife, Malka, and their three children, perished in Lithuania, probably in Mariampol, the city where they lived in according to testimony listed in Yad Vashem, the central database of victims of the *Shoah*. [10]

The experience of the Lithuanian Jews in relation to the two German occupations, World War I and World War II, was very similar to that of other Jewish populations in Eastern Europe. The fact that the experience during the first war was not the genocidal one of the second may have had something to do with the slow reaction of Jewish populations to rumors of Nazi atrocities as the German armies moved eastward during World War II. Of course, even if they did react

---

[10] http://www.yadvashem.org

appropriately, where would they have escaped to? Countries such as Canada were reluctant to admit Jewish refugees and in fact, as already noted in the last chapter, the Canadian response was just about the worst of any western nation. However, some Jews could have escaped the worst of the inferno that followed by making it into Soviet zones of control.

The first period of Lithuanian independence, from about 1922 to 1926, included the formation of a representative democracy. In 1926 a military takeover resulted in autocratic rule, which lasted until the Second World War. My mother and the bulk of her family left Lithuania for Canada in 1925, and so missed the downward spiral that followed.

Chapter 3: The Zionist Youth Movements (1925-1932)

Part 1: Ideologies

After 1925, the new Canadian arrivals who had been part of the *Hashomer* organization in Kishenev began to gravitate to a variety of different ideologies, primarily to left-wing Yiddish cultural movements and some even to the new Young Communist League. The reason was obvious. Some of the young immigrants had arrived directly from the Soviet Union of the mid-1920s, where they had already been young pioneers or, in the case of the older ones, members of a Russian Communist youth organization.[11] Many were exploited as workers in the sweatshops of the needle trade. And who were the exploiters? They were the earlier socialists, anarchists and Zionists, who had immigrated to Canada before World War I. One might ask why the young Jewish immigrants felt the need to leave the Garden of Eden; that is, Soviet Russia. The answer is simple: Children must follow their parents. The young Zionists came to Canada, rather than going to *Eretz Yisrael* (Palestine) for the same reason.

In 1926 the *Hashomer* organization became dominated by Lithuanian Jews,[12] who changed the program from that of a Zionist scout movement to a more pioneering, *chalutziut*, approach. This meant that members were expected to actually immigrate to Palestine ("make *aliyah*[13]") as they matured. In fact, due to an economic crisis

---

[11] Komsomols

[12] Litvaks

[13] Literally, in Hebrew, "to go up to Jerusalem".

in Palestine in the late 1920s, a number of Jews left Palestine[14] and immigrated to Canada. To many members of the *Hashomer* movement, the commitment to make *aliyah* was an abstract point just to be paid lip service. But Motl's Chienke and Chienke's Motl took it seriously and questioned their further association with *Hashomer Hatzair*. Motl's sister, Chaike, and others like her, were already shop workers in the needle trades. For them, the change to a left-wing ideology was simple. Chaike moved from *chalutziut* to a combination of trade unionism and Yiddish cultural revival. This was not the path for Motl and Chienke. They were still in school and not in the shops yet. And so they left *Hashomer*, reluctantly, and tried to find their own path.

One day, as Motl was doing his homework, one of Chaike's girlfriends asked if he would befriend her younger brother who had just arrived from Poland. Motl said, "Why not?" and, after meeting the brother, took him along to *Hashomer* functions. There, the brother, who was a little older, than Motl, began to agitate for a Marxist-Zionist youth movement of left-wing *Poale-Zion*[15] origin to which he had belonged in Poland. This approach, a combination of Zionism and Marxism, appealed to Motl and his close friends. At first they organized just a young cultural league; however, it became infiltrated by communists, who were obstructive and caused the group to be dissolved. At this point, Motl was joined by another friend who had arrived from Toronto. The newcomer was more mature, in addition to being a singer and a romantic. Together, with the leader of the Left-wing *Poale Zion* of America and a trade unionist from Toronto, a mass meeting was organized in Prince Arthur Hall, in Montreal. A Marxist-Zionist movement of the *Left Poale Zion* was formed. It consisted of

---

[14] Both then and today, Jews who leave Israel are referred to as yordim (Hebrew for "going down").

[15] Literally, in Hebrew, "workers of Zion".

Motl's friends, previous *Hashomer* members, as well as new immigrants who were arriving from Poland. Motl was promised that the new movement would also stand for *chalutziut* and would actively promote *aliyah* to Palestine.

Chienke experienced a similar course of events; however, she and other young immigrants organized a new right-wing *Poale Zion* socialist youth movement. The difference between the two wings was based on the degree of Marxism. Chienke consistently advised Motl that the *Left Poale Zion* movement was not the appropriate path for him.

Part 2: Motl's Trip to Western Canada

During the 1920s, the Jewish youth movements in Montreal were ideologically divided. Nevertheless, they were brought together in play and various sports activities on the slopes of Mount Royal and in ideological discussions in and around the Jewish Public Library. The friendship between Motl's Chienke and Chienke's Motl continued unbroken until the year 1928, when Motl began to push for an active commitment among the new Marxist-Zionists. But most of the members of the new organization were factory workers. They had to support their struggling families in Canada, or those members of their families who were still in Europe. To them the commitment to *chalutziut* was the movement's commitment. It did not involve them personally.

So Motl remained alone with his dream, with only the support and sympathy of his good friends, Chienke and Moishe, the new leader of the *Hashomer* movement. While Moishe shared Motl's dream, the *Hashomer* could do little in 1928. Motl, only eighteen years old, decided to volunteer as a laborer for the wheat harvest in Western Canada, along with another member of the Marxist-Zionist group, named Eli, who was about the same age as him. Until the invention of the combine, the farmers of the west were in desperate need of thousands of migrant workers to handle the summer and fall harvests. Eli was interested in joining Motl primarily because he was unemployed. He was well versed in the phraseology of the *Left Poale Zion,* and an excellent speaker, but he had no trade. He had immigrated to Montreal from Warsaw with his parents. His father was an old-fashioned Hebrew teacher. Eli saw an opportunity for change, in Motl's idea to volunteer for the western harvest.

Motl and Eli faced the problem of how to pay for their train trip to Winnipeg. Neither of them had any money. Motl drove a delivery truck for his brother Hershel's fruit business. He gave his weekly salary, fifteen dollars, to his parents to help sustain their grocery store. He could not expect his parents to pay the travel expenses for his adventures in Western Canada. Nor could he expect them to support his intention of learning to become a farmer so he could leave the family to become a *chalutz* (pioneer) in *Eretz Yisrael.* Eli faced the same opposition. Rochel, Motl's second-oldest sister, came to a youth group meeting to warn that she would lie down on the railroad tracks to prevent her youngest brother, Motl-le, from sacrificing himself for a life of hard labour.

Motl and Eli offered to work as assistants to a Jewish news agent for the three-day and three-night trip from Montreal to Winnipeg. Early one morning, with the help of friends, the two volunteers managed to get to the station before Rochel could carry out her threat. As Motl's family would not have anything to do with his adventures, Chienke offered to keep in touch through the mail. Moishe, the *Hashomer* leader, gave them a letter to give to a girl named Hadassah, the *Hashomer* leader in Winnipeg. For three days and three nights Motl and Eli sold the news agent's merchandise on the train. There was hardly any time for sleep. For their work, they received a free trip plus any tips that came their way.

The two young men stayed in Winnipeg for a few days. They met Hadassah and gave her Moishe's letter. She in turn introduced them to friends in *Hashomer,* who provided them with beds to sleep in at night. Eli was acquainted with local members of the *Left Poale Zion.* They looked at Motl and Eli as if to say, "You really take these things seriously?"

The two young men left Winnipeg and traveled further west, to Lethbridge, Alberta. This time it was at the expense of the Canadian Government, since the railway would take migrant workers from Winnipeg to the various Western communities for free. They observed the flat expanses of the prairies, with no woods and no lakes. It was the middle of June and the wheat was already grown. From the train window it looked like golden waves on a quiet sea. Motl was reminded of his hometown in the Ukraine, the same dry climate, but no villages and no gardens. All they could see were the train stations with wheat elevators and each farmer on his own homestead.

After two days and one night, they reached Medicine Hat. It was midnight Saturday and their train south to Lethbridge didn't leave until Sunday morning. They had no choice but to sleep on the floor of the station. But the two adventurers were so tired that they enjoyed a pleasant rest, one they would remember for the rest of their lives. Because it was Sunday, the selection bureau in Lethbridge was closed. By coincidence, they met a Jewish inhabitant, a man who was both the *shochet* (ritual slaughterer) and Hebrew teacher. Motl and Eli were invited to his home where they met a Jewish cattle buyer. The buyer advised them not to wait until the government bureau opened on Monday but rather to drive with him in his small car to the station town of Foremost, Alberta. There, they could apply for harvest work with the farmers that came to town to buy supplies. Motl and Eli accepted his advice and drove with him to Foremost. He left them at the station after inviting his two passengers to a Friday night Sabbath meal at his home in Winnipeg whenever they passed through on their way back to Montreal.

Alone in the station, Motl and Eli were at a loss as to what to do next. Walking by the town's single Chinese restaurant they noticed other (gentile) harvest workers eating huge steaks. Although they didn't know what kind of meat it was and it appeared to be only half cooked, they ate it anyway. Later they met other young harvest volunteers on the town's only street. These were young Doukhobors who were more experienced with itinerant farm work. At night they slept in rail cars that were empty and waited for the harvest. For food, they relied on potatoes from the fields around them, and wild ducks were cooked over bonfires. The two Jewish would-be workers joined them for one night.

The next morning, they met a farmer and offered their services. They were offered wages of four dollars a day plus board for the first two weeks when they would be stacking the bundles of cut wheat. On rainy days they would only receive board. Later, during the main threshing period, they would be paid six dollars a day. Motl and Eli accepted these conditions and began to work.

The work camp consisted of two bunkhouses on wheels that were moved from field to field with a tractor. One bunkhouse had enough beds for sixteen workers. The other contained a dining room, a kitchen, and an apartment for the Irish cook. The cook was a woman who was exceptionally kind to Motl and Eli, the youngest of the workers. The others were a mixed group of oddballs and adventurers, even poets. The ideals expressed by Motl and Eli were strange to them. The work was backbreaking and very hard on the two young men. The two-week stacking period went by, and the threshing was about to begin. When the farmer went back on his word and let them know that they would continue to be paid only four dollars a day because of their age, Motl and Eli decided to leave.

After collecting two weeks pay they were taken to another railway town, Bow Island, Alberta. There a young farmer agreed to pay them the full six dollars a day. The farm that he took them to was established by Norwegian immigrants at the turn of the twentieth century. On rainy days, the farmer's mother (his father had passed away some years earlier) described the hardships of early pioneering life, including the dugouts that they lived in at first. Under those conditions, they raised nine children, six of whom survived. The oldest was physically disabled due to polio. The remainder, a daughter and four sons, ran the 160-acre farm with their mother. A period of prosperity during the First World War made it possible for them to build a proper house and barn and buy modern equipment, including a windmill-driven pump for their well. The farmer's mother described the difficulties they experienced dealing with government bureaucrats and swindlers. She also said that thanks to a Jewish lawyer from

Chicago, the local farmers had been able to organize to buy and sell collectively to the station elevator.

The two young men worked hard. They rose at five every morning to feed and water the two huge horses. After breakfast in the house, they returned to the barn to harness the horses, ride them to the work camp in the field, and hitch them to an enormous wagon. Then they rode the wagon into the field and pitchforked the bundles of wheat into the wagon. They also had to take the wheat to the threshing machine and unload the wagon into the machine. The work went on from seven in the morning until seven at night. There were two short rest periods, a coffee break at ten in the morning and lunch at one in the afternoon.

The prairie nights were cold but the summer days were hot, and the men worked with their shirts off. In the evening, Motl and Eli rode the horses back to the barn, fed and watered them, and then returned to the house for supper. The farmer and his family were kind to them. They were allowed to sleep in the house instead of the barn, as was customary. They ate nourishing food. In fact, it turned out that the young men worked day and night, for all night they dreamt that they were throwing the sheaves of wheat from the field into the wagon and from the wagon into the threshing machine. Thank God for rainy days, when Motl and Eli could relax and discuss various matters amongst themselves as well as with the farmer and his family.

Motl and Eli talked about their personal experiences and their families. Eli was from Warsaw, a big city with a large Jewish population and many political and ideological rivalries. Motl's background was very different. He had experienced the somewhat naive and traditional Jewish life of a *shtetl* in the Ukraine. Much of his youth was spent in the *Hashomer* movement. Chienke, who had a perceptive mind, was right when she told Motl that the *Left Poale Zion* was not the place for him. Motl received mail regularly from Chienke, but not from his family.

One rainy day, the farmer's mother learned that Motl and Eli were from Montreal. She asked about a big church with steps, a place that sick and disabled people went to for miracle cures. She was referring to Saint Joseph's Oratory, a well-known Catholic pilgrimage site. The young men told her that they did not know much about the church because they were Jewish. The entire family, as well as the young teacher who boarded at the farm, were astonished. They found it difficult to believe that young Jewish men would be willing to do farm labour. The mother said that the only Jews she knew lived in Lethbridge. They were all in business or professional work. Motl and Eli had to explain that a Jewish proletariat existed in the larger Canadian cities and that the reason they were working on the farm was to prepare themselves for a pioneering life in the Holy Land. This was difficult for the listeners, with the possible exception of the teacher, to grasp.

Later, in mid-September, during the Jewish High Holy Day period, they saw a car coming down the dusty road. "Now," the mother said, "here comes a real Jew", a photographer from Lethbridge. During the spring he travelled among the farmers, collecting family snapshots, including pictures of family members who were no longer alive. He promised to return in the fall, when the farmers had cash, with a large portrait of the deceased. For this, he charged only three dollars. The photographer, a nice looking middle-aged man, came into the house and showed the family a large coloured portrait of their late husband and father. The portrait was framed and covered in glass. A mirror that could be hung on the wall opposite the portrait was included. The dead farmer's family was overwhelmed. However, when the mother offered the photographer his three dollars he refused to take it, saying it wasn't enough.

"But you said it would cost three dollars, last spring!" she exclaimed.

"Yes" said the photographer, "but that was without the colour and the glassed-in frame and the mirror so you can see your late husband everywhere."

The mother began to bargain, offering five, then ten and then fifteen dollars. Finally she said "how much do you want?"

"Twenty-five dollars" was the reply. When the mother protested that they hadn't planned on spending that much, the photographer began to remove the portrait. At this, the family relented. They could not let the photographer leave with the portrait, and so they paid him the twenty-five dollars.

Now the mother said to the photographer "we have a different kind of Jewish people here with us." And she pointed to Motl and Eli. "They worked hard with us all summer and now they will travel to the Holy Land to help create a new Jewish working society." The astonished photographer asked if they were really Jewish and when they replied in the affirmative, he offered to take them to town on *Yom Kippur*. Motl and Eli refused, saying that they would rather stay at the farm, although they would not work on *Yom Kippur*.

In November Motl and Eli prepared to leave the hard-working farmer and his family. They had each earned three hundred and fifty dollars, a very sizable sum, in their minds. At first they planned to undertake further adventures: perhaps a trip to Banff and the Rockies and later to Vancouver and Victoria? But then they realized that they were lonesome for home. Motl especially. He wanted to see Chienke, to tell her about his experiences and to show her how fit and muscular he had become. They travelled east, following their outward route, stopping in Winnipeg to visit friends and to spend Friday evening with the cattle buyer who had befriended them earlier in the summer. The buyer and his family were impressed with the serious and idealistic nature of the two young Jews from Montreal.

Motl's family welcomed him back to Montreal. His brother Hershel hired him back into his fruit business and took him shopping for clothing more appropriate for an adult. Motl's father tried to turn him away from further adventures. He wanted Motl to become an independent businessman like his brother. Since a truck was too expensive, Motl was set up business with a horse and wagon. But with *chalutziut* on his mind, Motl's career in business didn't last long. He went back to work for his brother. He also took evening courses in mechanics and blueprint reading at the Montreal Technical School, as further preparation for a pioneering life. Motl gave up his association with the Marxist youth movement and moved closer to Chienke's way of thinking, but in the end, Chienke's *Poale Zion* group dissolved.

Part 3: Youth Leadership in Montreal

In the year 1929 the Jewish community in Canada faced a severe economic crisis brought on by poverty and unemployment. Soup kitchens became commonplace. The political situation for Jews became tense as well. Pogroms carried out by Arabs against Jews in Hebron and Safed, in Palestine, alarmed the Jews of Canada. That such a thing should happen in *Eretz Yisrael* was unacceptable. Chienke and Motl took part in protest marches. Motl and some of his friends joined Jewish war veterans who wanted to organize a Jewish Legion to fight the Arabs, but nothing came of it.

In this troubled time, Motl became friends with Berl and David, two former members of the dissolved *Right Poale Zion* group, the same group that Chienke had joined earlier. Together, they began to plan for the organization of a new *chalutz* movement that would not only be directed at immigrant youth but also the Jewish youth born in Canada. They needed the right leadership, and Motl knew that his best friend Chienke was the best person for the job. He made an appointment to see her on Mount Royal on Sunday. They walked for hours. It was drizzling, and they both got soaking wet. Motl took Chienke to a special fruit store on Laurier Avenue, where she tasted honeydew for the first time. Their discussion about a new youth movement ended on the steps of her home on Saint Urbain Street, when Chienke's brother-in-law Yossel opened the door and said, "Come in out of the rain before you catch cold."

With Chienke's special knowledge and talent, and with the cooperation of leading senior[16] and junior members of the *Poale Zion*

---

[16] For example, Belkin, Cheifitz and Bobrov.

movement, the formation of a new youth organization began to gather momentum. Most of the organizational work was carried out by the quartet of Motl and his friends, Berl, David and Yesoschar. Chienke provided educational leadership, assisted by two teachers: Libbe-Shaindel and Kalman, as well as by volunteers from the Gordonia organization, a non-Marxist Zionist youth movement founded in 1923 and based on the writings and philosophy of the well-known Hebrew writer, A. D. Gordon.

First, a new Yiddish club for new immigrants was formed. Next, Kalman and Yesoschar organized the English-speaking youth. But the largest task involved the development of an organization for Canadian-born children. The first group, organized for girls, was named after Sarah Chizhik, a *Hechalutz* heroine who died with Yosef Trumpeldor and six others in the defense of Tel Chai in upper Galilee. This successful group was Chienke's achievement. It was, and remains many years later, a central feature of the Montreal Labour Zionist scene. It is a current source of leadership for the Naamat organization, a worldwide charity and progressive women's organization dedicated to improving family life in Israel and elsewhere. Chienke also helped Yesoschar organize a group for boys, named Yehoash—the name of the Yiddish translator of the Bible. This involved a trip to Lachine, a Montreal suburb, in Yesoschar's panel truck. Kalman, who was a student at McGill University, was entrusted with leading this group.

All this organizational activity had a lasting effect on the Labour Zionist movement. The winter of 1931-32 represented the starting point and involved the setting up a summer camp to provide *chalutziut* experience for children. This was Motl and Chienke's idea. It required the material assistance of senior members of the *Poale Zion*, such as *Chaver*[17] Zelick, who owned a dress factory. Zelick, assisted by his capable wife, had worked hard to create his factory. In spite of being a successful manufacturer, he remained committed to the socialist ideals of his youth. Many members of the *Poale Zion*

---

[17] Comrade; or, literally, in Hebrew, "friend".

youth movement were given jobs in his factory. As it happens, a strike in the lady's garment industry pitted these same members against their own *chaver*, Zelick. At a meeting of the *Poale Zion* they asked for Zelick's expulsion from the organization. However, Motl and other loyal friends could not accept such behaviour and the matter nearly came to blows, particularly between Motl and his friend Moishe. Fortunately, the strike ended and Zelick was able to help Motl and his associates, Belkin, Berl, David and Yesoschar, to establish a camp in the Laurentian Mountains, just north of Montreal. They rented a large farmhouse beside a stream. This was the beginning of Undzer[18] Camp, one of the best-known and most successful summer camps to be established around Montreal.

The camp was organized on a charitable and educational basis to provide a summer vacation opportunity for poorer Jewish children. Gitel, an experienced teacher from the Peretz School, named after the famed nineteenth and early twentieth centry Yiddish author, I.L. Peretz, was chosen to be the camp mother. The cook was a widow whose two children were enrolled in the camp free of charge. There was no difficulty in attracting interest in the camp. The campers, included children of parents belonging to the various Labour Zionist groups, particularly those of the older *Poale Zion* members and students attending the Peretz School and the Jewish People's School (Folkshul). These schools emphasized secular Jewish education and Yiddish, in contrast to the more religious program of Talmud Torah schools.

For Chienke and Motl and the other organizers, the summer camp was designed to further the goals of the movement. It was decided that Chienke would become the second camp counselor. David volunteered to be in charge of camp services, while Motl, Yesoschar and others gave resources and their time to the camp on weekends. The establishment of the camp was one of the principal

---

[18] Literally, "our camp".

achievements of the Labour Zionist movement. It also gave Chienke an opportunity to demonstrate her ability as an educator and leader.

At the end of the summer of 1931, the renewed American and Canadian *Poale Zion* youth movement organized a convention in Toronto for the purpose of developing a more pioneering orientation, as originally proposed by Motl and Chienke. With a view to attracting larger numbers of youth born in Canada and the United States, the name was changed to *Habonim.*[19] A large number of Montreal delegates attended, including Motl and Chienke, but the organization could only afford to pay the expenses of one delegate, Chienke. The fact that Chienke was chosen because of her role in organizing the summer camp was very satisfying to Motl.

The convention was a period of great excitement and activity, including singing and dancing. Those watching from the sidelines must have thought that the world was going to be turned upside down by these young men and women. A new camp was established in Detroit during the convention. A training farm to prepare for a pioneering life had already been founded in Hightown, New Jersey.

In her role as secretary of *Hechalutz*, Montreal, Chienke had corresponded with Moishe Solovaitchik, the convention delegate from Hightown. Moishe arrived in a truck with the delegation from Washington D.C. Motl's meeting with Moishe made an impression on him, and he decided to leave the convention with Moishe to go directly to the training farm in New Jersey. Chienke advised Motl to return to Montreal and help organize a training programme[20] there, but Motl had no patience. After asking Chienke to take his extra belongings back to his parents in Montreal, Motl left the convention with Moishe and the Washington delegates. When their truck reached

---

[19] In Hebrew, "the builders".

[20] Hachshara

Niagara Falls it was midnight. When asked by the border guard where he was going, Motl, who didn't have proper documents, replied, "To see the Falls from the American side." The guard pointed out that the lights illuminating the falls had been turned off. He advised Motl to go back to Canada and return to see the Falls the next morning. The group could not wait, so Motl had no alternative but to hitchhike back to Montreal.

While hitchhiking, Motl encountered two convention delegates from New York. Both were named Benny. The two Bennys, who were travelling to Ottawa and Montreal on their way home, talked Motl into joining them[21]. When they arrived in Montreal the three young men had a joyful reunion with Chienke and with Motl's family.

Part 4: Motl Prepares to Make Aliyah

Motl's experience at the Habonim convention convinced him to prepare himself to make *aliyah* to *Eretz Yisrael*. First, he had to obtain a passport. While Motl's immigration papers indicated that he was 21 years old, in fact he was only 19. Motl's parents were not happy to see their son leave Canada for a hard life in Palestine. When they complained to a *landsman,*[22] he told them to be happy that they had son who was an idealist. The *landsman* went with Motl to the records department at city hall where he swore an affidavit to the effect that Motl was 21 years old and therefore entitled to obtain his own passport.

---

[21] Coincidentally, Motl and one the Bennys met later on in Palestine while working at the Ruttenberg power station on the Jordan River. At that time Motl was a member of Kibbutz Gesher while Benny was from Kibbutz Affikim.

[22] A fellow immigrant from their home town.

That same year (1931-32), Motl enrolled once again in practical engineering courses at Montreal Technical School, a trade school that opened in 1911 and that is now a part of the Université du Québec à Montréal, for more training. Chienke tried to convince Motl to wait one year so she could go with him. Also, she thought, it might be possible to organize a group for *aliyah*. But Motl explained that he was afraid of losing momentum and he could not wait any longer. It was agreed between them that Chienke would join Motl in one year in *Eretz Yisrael*, regardless of whether a group went with her or not. Motl promised to arrange a spot on a kibbutz for Chienke, while she promised to maintain contact with him during their one-year separation.

Meanwhile, the Canadian economic crisis continued. Communist influence gained strength in the winter of 1931-32. The Communists prepared large May Day demonstrations. Senior figures in the socialist movement agreed to a demand from the youth wing to prepare a leaflet describing the socialist agenda. The youth were asked to distribute it to the masses. Motl and two younger girls from Chienke's group were passing out leaflets on St. Laurent Street, when a policeman grabbed Motl's arms. The two girls ran away. Motl told the policeman that he was not a communist, but it didn't help. Motl was placed in a police wagon with communists and vagrants and taken to the station. The two girls ran to their organizational headquarters to tell others what had happened. At about midnight, *Chaver* Bobrov, a lawyer, came to the station to get Motl released on bail. Motl finally returned to his waiting and nervous parents at 2 a.m. At the trial, the Communists pleaded not guilty but still received jail sentences. Fortunately, when the lawyer explained the policeman's error to the judge in that Motl was not a Communist, Motl was excused from having to stand trial.

In later years, Bovrov enjoyed telling the story of Motl's arrest. A Yiddish Communist weekly published in Toronto reported that innocent communists were sentenced to jail while a social democrat, namely Motl, was not even brought to trial for doing the same thing. The newspaper's editor was Bovrov's acquaintance. When they met, the lawyer asked how the paper could publish such rubbish.

The editor replied that he was surprised that Bovrov read such a rag of a paper!

Some weeks later, the second day of *Shavuot*, a holiday which commemorates the day that God gave the Torah to Moses and the Israelites, Motl was to board a ship in the Port of Montreal to take him to *Eretz Yisrael* to begin a new pioneering life. The night before he left, Motl and Chienke had a serious discussion about their common goals and ideals. Chienke promised to see Motl off at the dock and to bring him a special package. The secretary of the *Poale Zion* movement also gave Motl a special package and asked him to deliver it into the hands of the secretary of the Histadrut Labour Federation, in Palestine. The package was sewn into the lining of Motl's jacket.

Motl's family was reconciled to his *aliyah* to *Eretz Yisrael*. Because it was Shavuot, Motl's parents and their *Poale Zion landsman* walked four miles to the port. His brother Hershel and his wife and their baby son, Bernard, along with sister Chaike and her friends, and his sister Odel and her husband (and his mother), were at the dock. Many others were there as well, including the principal of the *Folkshul* and friends from the youth groups. Photographs were taken, but Chienke wasn't in any of the pictures. Where was Chienke? She appeared only after Motl was on the ship and it had begun to move. The school principal threw her package to Motl on the ship. Motl yelled down, "Why did you come so late?" She answered by saying that she would write him a special letter. Chienke didn't want anyone to witness the feelings that existed between them.

Jacob's Commentary

This chapter of my parent's memoirs emphasizes the ideological ferment that enveloped the Jewish youth of their day and the extent to which they were caught up in the minutia and nuanced variations between the various, mostly left wing, groups. For example, how much difference can there be between the Left or Right Poale Zion organizations, given that both are labour- (workers of Zion) oriented? Yet those involved were passionately devoted to their cause and believed that they could change the world. Much of the ideology was directed toward the development of communal agricultural settlement, the kibbutz, in Palestine.

It is important to note that while these memoirs concentrate on the left wing movements, Jewish political activity at that time included the entire spectrum of ideologies, including the Bund, a non-Zionist Jewish Labour movement that was popular in Eastern Europe (mainly Lithuania, Russia and Poland), as well as the Revisionist Zionists, led by the charismatic Zeev Jabotinsky. The revisionists were a nationalist group that focused on the establishment of a Jewish majority in Palestine in as large a territory as possible. This was Menachem Begin's background and the Likud Party of Israel is a descendent of this political movement. The revisionists and their youth wing, Betar, were very popular in Poland

The Poale Zion movement developed in the early 1900s, both in Europe and in the United States and Canada. Ber Borochov, the Marxist Zionist founder of the movement believed that class struggle and Jewish Nationalism were not mutually exclusive. He believed that Arab and Jewish workers would join forces once the Jews returned to Palestine. When I think back to my father's comments to me on this and later phases of his life, it is clear that Borochov was his ideological hero. Borochov died in Russia in 1917 after returning from the United States in order to organize Jewish forces from Poale Zion members to fight for the red army.

The split into right and left Poale Zion factions occurred in 1919, the right wing being non-Marxist and less radical than the left. *Gordonia*, a pioneering Zionist youth movement that is referred to in this chapter, was based on the writings of Aaron David Gordon. Founded in Poland, this movement viewed itself as being less elitist than *Hashomer*, but its prime focus on *aliyah* to Palestine and on the development of kibbutz life were, to my mind, very similar. In fact, it is really difficult to see much if any difference between *Hashomer*, the right *Poale Zion* and the *Gordonia* movements. All of them were primarily active in the period between the two World Wars. During and after World War II and the establishment of the State of Israel, the various movements evolved or morphed into new entities or became part of the Israeli political landscape. *Gordonia* merged with *Habonim*, yet another Zionist youth movement referred to by my parents. *Poale Zion* in North America joined with the *Farband* (the Jewish National Workers Alliance) to form the *Labor Zionist Alliance*.

The numbers of individuals that actually attended the various meetings that my parents refer to were quite small, often less than 40, but the organizations had a global scope in that their origins were usually European. For the most part, it was the Jewish immigrants who brought these ideologies to North America, particularly the teenagers, such as my parents. I don't think that my parents understood that their perception was related to their experiences and the times in which they lived. While my sister did belong to various Zionist youth organizations when she was in her teens, I didn't. Nor did any of my friends, even though we attended a Jewish day school with a Zionist orientation, in which 50% of the curriculum was in Hebrew. I did join the youth wing of the B'nai Brith organization in my later teens. However, this was for social reasons only and the organization was not at all ideological, at least at that time. I know that my parents wondered what young people do with themselves in the absence of an ideological sense of purpose and I can recall that their wonder extended to my children as well, when my children were older and could interact with them.

This chapter also points out that while numerous individuals were caught up in these ideological movements, very few actually did anything about it. While Palestine, and later Israel, attracted millions of Jewish immigrants during the twentieth century, the number who actually left their homes purely on the basis of Zionist principles, and not for reasons of personal safety or economics, is likely very small. In the Diaspora, groups such as the *Farband* became fraternal benefit societies involved in mutual aid, charity fund raising and organizing social events. My parents became more involved in such activities as they reestablished their lives in Montreal upon their return from Palestine. In spite of their youthful and Utopian socialist ideals, most of my father's friends became businessmen, just as he ultimately did. Nevertheless, they always addressed each other in a formal manner, using their surnames, preceded by the word "*Chaver*" (Hebrew for friend, or in the socialist style, comrade). Both of my parents were buried in the Farband section of a large Jewish cemetery in Montreal.

Two important historical events are mentioned briefly in this chapter, and both merit further elaboration. First, mention is made of Trumpeldor, Sarah Chizhik and the defense of Tel Chai. Joseph Trumpeldor was a Russian Jew who fought for Russia in the Russian Japanese War of 1905. He was cited for bravery under fire, (losing an arm in the process) and was promoted to Officer, the first Jewish officer in the Russian army. During World War I he was instrumental in the establishment of the Zion Mule Corps, the first all-Jewish fighting force in almost two thousand years, and he was wounded again at the battle of Gallipoli. He was also founder of *Hehalutz,* a youth movement mentioned elsewhere. Trumpeldor immigrated to Palestine in 1918, and became a Jewish national hero when he died in 1920, along with seven others, defending Tel Chai, a Jewish settlement in northern Galilee, from Lebanese Arab marauders. It is reputed that his dying words were, "It is good to die for our country". Sarah Chizhik, a sister of Hannah Chizhik, who was a pioneer in the development of agricultural training for women, and who Motl met early after his arrival in Palestine, died alongside Trumpeldor.

The other events that should be described further are the pogroms that took place in Safed and Hebron in 1929. The pogroms were related to anti-Zionist riots instigated by the Palestinian Arab leadership, especially by the Grand Mufti of Jerusalem. It has been noted that 67 Jews were killed in Hebron and 18 in Safed. Many more were injured. The pogroms had a devastating effect on those Jews in the Diaspora who were contemplating making *aliyah* to Palestine. Ironically, the Jewish communities affected the most, Hebron and Safed, were primarily religious communities that had existed, along with those of Jerusalem and Tiberius, for centuries. This serves to highlight the fact that during the nearly 2000 years between the destruction of the second temple and the establishment of the modern state of Israel, the Land of Israel was never devoid of a Jewish population. While the Jewish population during the period of Ottoman rule may have been a minority in terms of the whole country, there is evidence that Jews formed a majority of the city of Jerusalem from at least the mid-1800s. Moreover, pogroms in locations such as Safed took place at other times in history, well before the start of modern Zionist settlement in Palestine.

Chapter 4: Eretz Yisrael

Part 1: Motl's Journey

When the ship started to move out of the Montreal harbour in June, 1932, Motl was at last on his way to fulfilling his commitment to *aliyah* and to kibbutz life. The trip down the St. Lawrence River and across the Atlantic to Le Havre, France took seven days. The ship's passengers were mainly European immigrants who had become disillusioned with life in Canada and in the United States, and were returning to their fatherlands. This was common in the years following the stock market crash of 1929. Motl also felt that he was returning to his fatherland. He and a Chassidic emissary were the only Jews on board. Motl had little interest or language in common with most of the other passengers and so he spent a good deal of his time reflecting on what he had left behind and on his expectations concerning *Eretz Yisrael*.

Motl's family and friends, especially Chienke, were left behind in Montreal. However, he could count on Chienke's promise to join him in kibbutz life in one year. Moreover, there were a number of contacts to be made and individuals he wanted to meet. Before he left Montreal, Golde, a neighbour who knew his mother and his sister, Rochel, gave Motl her sister's address on Ben Yehuda Street in Tel Aviv and suggested that he spend his first few days in Eretz Yisrael at her home. Tel Aviv was also the location of the office of the secretary of the *Histadrut*, the General Federation of Labor, the contact who was to receive the package given to Motl by the *Poale Zion* Party in Montreal. Chienke told Motl not to forget to visit Sarah from Winnipeg, who was on Chana Chizek's farm for girls, near Tel Aviv. Also, Motl's *chaver* Yehuda, in Montreal, made him promise to visit Givat Brenner, a kibbutz he had helped found near Rohovot. In addition, Motl knew of a group of Montreal *Hashomer* members who had settled in Kibbutz Mishmar Ha-Emek one year earlier. That group included some *chaverim* from New York who were originally from the *Hashomer* movement in Kishenev.

There were also family connections to make. Motl's mother's family in the town of Ternivke had also escaped the pogroms in the Ukraine. They too were stranded as refugees in Romania, but instead of trying to reach America or Canada they had settled in Eretz Yisrael. There, with the help of American relatives, they bought wagons and mules and various implements with which to start a business in the Hadar Hacarmel section of Haifa. Motl also knew that he had a cousin, Ada, in Kfar Giladi and another cousin, Chana, in Metulla.

The list of friends and contacts continued. There was Moishe, who had befriended Motl at the *Habonim* convention in Toronto and who had made *aliyah* with others from Detroit. And then there was Zalman, a Hebrew teacher from Montreal who had settled a year earlier in a new kibbutz, Ramat Yochanan, located near Haifa Bay. Finally, Motl had assisted two *Moshav*[23] movement emissaries, Shimon from Kfar Yechezkel and Tzvi from Nahalal, when they had visited Montreal. They both invited Motl to visit them when he arrived in *Eretz Yisrael*.

Motl had seven days and nights to think and to plan as he sailed across the ocean. He was reminded of the yearnings and emotions for the land of his forefathers expressed in the poetry of Yehuda Halevi, the famous fourteenth century Jewish writer. Halevi travelled to *Eretz Yisrael* on a sailing ship, crossing the Mediterranean from west to east. Motl travelled by steamship, also from west to east, across the Atlantic. From Le Havre, he planned to travel overland to Paris and Trieste, and then spend four days on another ship to the port of Jaffa in Palestine.

Although Motl expected to settle in Eretz Yisrael permanently, immigration restrictions imposed by the British Mandatory Government had reduced the number of entry certificates available. Motl entered Palestine on a tourist visa with the intention of never leaving. In fact, he managed to lose his passport, although fortunately

---

[23] Settlements in which labour is communal but property remains private.

not his Canadian citizenship papers. After paying for the various portions of his trip, Motl was left with the worldly sum of one hundred dollars!

The trip from Montreal to Jaffa lasted seventeen days.In addition to the Atlantic crossing, Motl spent three days in Paris, a couple of nights in Trieste and a day in Cyprus. While he was in Paris he rode the Metro and visited the Eiffel tower. Motl had little money to spend, but in the early 1930s, the dollar was king and a complete meal cost only ten cents. When eating a meal in a restaurant one day, Motl was astonished to find himself being serenaded by a violinist on bended knee wearing a Charlie Chaplin style suit. Motl could not understand how a talented person who could play such inspiring music could lower himself in this way. When Motl gave him a dollar the musician thanked him profusely and tried to kiss his hand. Motl pulled his hand away and said that the money was for the quality of his playing and nothing more.

The train to Trieste stopped in Turin, where it was boarded by a pleasant young man who sat down next to Motl. They began to chat. The newcomer said he was a Jew and an anti-fascist and he could even speak a few words of Hebrew. Motl took him at his word and freely expressed his own views about Mussolini's Italy. In Milan, Motl's new friend left the train and was replaced by an unfriendly man with fascist leanings who appeared to be a police agent. This man followed Motl until he arrived in Trieste and boarded the ship that would take him to *Eretz Yisrael*.

The ship that Motl boarded in Trieste to cross the Adriatic and Mediterranean Seas was smaller than the one that carried him across the Atlantic. All of the passengers were Jewish.They included families from Poland, who were travelling as tourists but who planned to remain in Palestine. These people had the foresight to escape the anti-semitism of Poland. In addition, there were groups of experienced *chalutzim* with legal entry certificates as well as Palestinian university students (the term Palestinians was used mainly to describe Jews at this time and until the early 1950s) who were returning from Europe for their summer vacations, and kibbutz emissaries[24] who were returning home. Finally, some young Polish *chalutzim* without proper documents arrived in Trieste on bicycles and were smuggled on board by paying passengers, including Motl. When the ship arrived at Jaffa, the stowaways swam ashore at night and became a part of the permanent population.

The five days Motl spent on the ship was a happy and lively time. All kinds of Jews were returning to Eretz Yisrael. Motl tried to befriend the *chalutzim* from Europe, but they didn't really believe that he intended to become a part of *chalutz* life. He was only accepted by Menachem, who was from *Kibbutz Gesher*. Menachem was returning from Vienna, where he had undergone medical treatment. As fate would have it, Motl, and later Chienke, ended up spending five years in Gesher, along with their daughter, who was born there. Motl wanted to join in the activities of the more experienced *chalutzim*, but they ignored him.

Part 2: Motl Looks for a Place to Settle Down

When the ship arrived at Jaffa, passengers and cargo were transferred to land in lighters, small boats used to transfer passengers and cargo from ships to shore, rowed by Arabs, to the accompaniment of much shouting and yelling. In fact, Jaffa was almost a completely Arab city. Was this *Eretz Yisrael*? To get to Tel Aviv, a city with a Jewish population of 40,000, Motl had to hire a horse drawn cart driven by an Arab. It didn't take long to get to Ben Yehuda Street where Golde's sister lived and where he received an encouraging welcome. Motl asked his hostess how he could reach the Secretary of the *Histadrut*, to give him the special package that had been sewn into

---

[24] Shlichim (Zionist emissaries)

the lining of his jacket. She referred him to an acquaintance, who suggested that Motl turn the package over to him so he could deliver it. This, Motl would not do. He made his way to the *Histadrut* building by himself. There, the doorman indicated that the Secretary was a busy man and that Motl should hand the package over to him. Motl insisted on waiting. After waiting and observing the people and bureaucratic operations of the office, Motl was finally shown into the Secretary's office. After providing proof of Motl's identity, he accepted Motl's package. This, it turned out, contained $5000, an amount equivalent to more than ten times that amount today.

The Secretary was grateful and, thinking that Motl was a tourist, offered to arrange a tour for him along with other important visitors. Showing the Secretary his knapsack, Motl explained that he planned to walk or hitchhike from kibbutz to kibbutz until he found a suitable place to settle and prepare for Chienke's arrival.

"So what can I do for you?" asked the Secretary. Motl replied that he would like a letter of introduction that he could use when he visited the various settlements. The Secretary dictated a letter immediately.

Motl mentioned that he planned to visit Sarah, his and Chienke's friend from Winnpeg. Sarah was at a woman's workers farm organized by the famous Hannah Chizhik, which was located in the northern outskirts of Tel Aviv. The Secretary told Motl that his wife was also from Winnipeg and that she knew Sarah. He gave Motl directions to the farm and asked him to invite Hannah and her husband as well as Sarah to join Motl and other guests at a party at his home. The party was to be held in honour of David Pinski, a well-known Yiddish writer who was visiting *Eretz Yisrael* with his wife.

On the bus to the woman's farm, Motl thought he recognized the writer Pinski. In fact, the writer and his wife had been invited to visit the farm. The three of them got off the bus at the last stop. From there it was a half hour lonely walk across a vast expanse of sand dunes to the farm. The older couple was glad to have Motl's company. Despite the difference in age (Pinski was about 65) the three of them got along very well. Motl explained that he knew the writer from his books and from his visits to Montreal.

Hannah Chizhik was pleased to see them when they finally arrived at their destination. At first she thought that Motl was the couple's grandson. When she found out that Motl was there to visit Sarah, she asked him if he would mind going into the field to tell Sarah and the thirty-five other young women to leave their work and return to the house to greet the important visitors. At the house, Motl sat at the head of the table with the two other visitors. After some refreshments, Pinski read one of his stories. He read so naturally and in such a normal tone that when he uttered the sentence,"Hannah, bring me a glass of water," the hostess, Hannah ran to the kitchen to bring him a drink. That same evening Hannah and her husband, along with the Pinskis and Motl and Sarah, went to the gathering at the home of the Secretary.

The next morning Motl left Tel Aviv and walked in the direction of Rehovot, by way of the then agricultural settlements of Nes Tziona and Rishon Le-Zion, until he reached Kibbutz Givat Brenner. He was overwhelmed by the sight of the groves of fruit and the fields of produce. These were examples of the agricultural potential envisioned in modern Zionism. At Givat Brenner, Motl presented his letter of introduction and the greetings of *Chaver* Yehuda of Montreal to the Kibbutz Secretary, who was ill in bed. Motl was referred to Yehuda's friends who, it happens, were also sick. They wondered why Motl had left Canada, and one bed-ridden *chaver* called him an idiot.

Motl began to understand the hardships of kibbutz life in 1932. The kibbutz had only 500 dunams of land from the Jewish National Fund at its disposal. Many of the chavers worked outside the kibbutz, either as domestics or in the fields of the well-to-do private farmers, or in the building trade. They had to do outside work to survive because the funds the kibbutz received from the Jewish Agency were insufficient.The budget for food per person per day was only two piasters: about ten cents.

It was depressing, but it didn't discourage Motl. He went on to the next kibbutz, Givat Hashlosha, near the town of Petach Tikva. When he handed his letter of introduction to the kibbutz secretary, in the hut that served as an office, he was asked if he was born in

Canada. When Motl explained that he was originally from the town of Monastrishch in the Ukraine, the man exclaimed that he was from the neighbouring town of Uman. In fact, he knew Motl's sister Rochel who had studied there! Then he told Motl that another kibbutz *chaver*, Avram Zradonovsky, was also from Monastrishch. At this news Motl cried out, "He is my cousin!"

The two cousins met at Avram's hut. Avram, who was older than Motl, had been a friend of Motl's sisters, Sarah and Rochel. He had last seen Motl when Motl was ten years old. Avram tried to encourage Motl to settle at his kibbutz. The kibbutz was poor and the living conditions were hard, but the *chaverim* were planning to buy a truck, and they needed someone like Motl who knew how to drive. Motl refused to stay. He told his friends that that he had a mission to locate a site not only for himself to live, but for others who were coming later.

Motl's next stop was Mishmar Ha-Emek, where *Hashomer Hatzair* friends from Montreal and New York had settled a year earlier. Although his friends were still living in tents, Motl was encouraged by the appearance of a more established kibbutz. He stayed for a whole month, working in the fields and even getting involved in a fight with Arab shepherds. His friend Moishe, from New York, and his friend Schmuel, from Montreal, tried to convince Motl to stay. Motl and Schmuel's friendship went back to when they were refugees in Kishinev in 1921. Only Motl's ideological concerns made him decide to wait.

Motl took a holiday from visiting *kibbutzim* to spend some time with his family. First, he visited his Uncle Schmuel-Abba in Hadar Ha-Carmel, Haifa. There, he experienced a different, more middle class perspective of life in *Eretz Yisrael*. In a different way, these people were also pioneers. When they arrived in 1921, they encountered an undeveloped society. They received a plot of land as a free loan from the Jewish American Society. Using their mules, wagons and tents they established a small transportation company for the building trade. With the money they earned, they slowly built a home and a store on their plot of land. Turkish law, which was still in effect during the British Mandate, stipulated that long-term occupancy of public land could be used to claim ownership, provided that a building—including a roof—was erected. Motl's uncle and two cousins had done just that. At the time of Motl's visit they had become full owners of the land. Two grocery stores, one for each of the cousins and their families, were established on the ground floor of their building. Motl's uncle and aunt, as well as a widowed sister and her two children, lived in the basement. The original huts that they lived in were either rented or used by needy families.

Motl's family had decided to add a floor to the main building. Motl's uncle said, "If you really want to be a pioneer, help us with this construction." Motl agreed and that became his first experience in the building trade. Motl worked for two weeks helping to finish the cement roof. Instead of getting a real salary, his cousin Refael gave him small slips of paper inscribed with his signature and an amount.

"What kind of money is this?" asked Motl. The cousin explained that the lack of adequate banking made a kind of barter system necessary. The suppliers of building materials were paid with the same pieces of paper. They in turn used these bits of paper to pay their workers and the workers used them to buy goods in the cousins' stores.

"So what should I do with them?" asked Motl.

"Keep them as a souvenir," replied his cousin.

Another experience that Motl had in Haifa involved the time his cousin Leibel took him to the port, which at that time was quite primitive. They stole out of the house on a Saturday so his uncle would not know that they were breaking the Sabbath. Their destination was an old ship and dock where the *Haganah*, an illegal Jewish paramilitary organization, was conducting training exercises under the guise of sports activities run by the local Hapoal sports club. This was Motl's first military experience. He was told that his participation that day made him a member of the *Haganah*. In the evening the entire group marched through the old downtown section of Haifa carrying lighted torches and singing a ribald song about a girl looking for sailors on the beach: "God will not forgive us because we played with the waves and we became angels." This was a show of strength to the

Arab population and to the ultra-orthodox Jews who were against the breaking of the Sabbath.

The next morning Motl was on his way to the new kibbutz of Ramat Yohanan. This was the home of Zalman, the Hebrew teacher from Montreal, and Moishe, the *chaver* from Detroit, who Motl met at the *Habonim* convention in Toronto. Motl stayed there for three months.

Ramat Yohanan was, at that time, a temporary settlement established by a group of graduates of Mikveh Israel, an agricultural school, who were camping in the vicinity of Kibbutz Ginnegar. The group from Detroit arrived in 1931. The members of the settlement had not yet decided which kibbutz movement to belong to. Most of them had an overly romantic view of kibbutz life, which Motl was still too naive to realize.

When Motl left his family in Haifa to go to Ramat Yohanan, he walked in the direction of the Nesher cement factory until he arrived at Kibbutz Yagur. Then he turned in the direction of Kfar Chasidim. It was a very hot day. A Jewish policeman stopped him and asked where he was going. When Motl replied that he was walking to the Northern Settlement (as Ramat Yohanan was then known) the policeman said, "Are you crazy? Look at you, you're all swollen from the heat. I am a member of that group and it is still four kilometres away. Come, I'll take you there on my horse." Together, they rode into the settlement.

Zalman and Moishe were of course very surprised to see Motl. They did their best to accommodate him under difficult circumstances, even sharing a bed. The settlement was located in a barren landscape. The members lived in an abandoned Arab compound built in the Middle Ages. The compound, made of stone walls and tiled roof, included an old-fashioned well, where they showered by holding a water pail with holes in the bottom over each other's head. The men and women in the group were supposed to shower separately, but there were accidents!

At the time of Motl's arrival, the group had decided to demolish the old structure and build a new one. Motl participated in this work. However, the settlement needed funds to continue to exist, and the Jewish Agency had no funds to spare. As a result, some of the members had to work outside the settlement in the developing industrial basin of the Zebulon Valley around Haifa Bay. They worked for the Jewish National Fund where the towns of Kiryat[25] Atta, Kiryat Haim, Kiryat Bialik and Kiryat Motzkin are now found. The work, which Motl did too, involved draining the Kishon River and surrounding swamps. They worked during the day, while evenings were reserved for serious discussions concerning the future direction of their new lifestyle.

One day, Zalman, the former Hebrew teacher from Montreal, took Motl aside and advised him that he would be better off in the non-elitist United Kibbutz Movement. To investigate this possibility Motl decided to travel to Kibbutz Ein Harod in the Jezreel Valley and then walk to the nearby *kibbutzim*. He got as far as a small settlement near Nahalal by hitching a ride on a horse-drawn wagon. There, Motl, who arrived sick with fever, rested and recuperated. From there he planned to travel to Kfar Yechezkel to visit his friend Shimon. This portion of the trip took two days and involved passing through the kibbutz settlements of Sarid, Ginnegar, and Mizra, where he spent the night. From there he passed Tel Adashim, Afula, then, just a train station, and Merchavia.[26] Finally he arrived at Kfar Yechezkel, where he stayed for the night with Shimon and his family.

Shimon introduced Motl to a fellow member of his moshav, named Tillman. Motl said that the Hebrew teacher in his hometown in the Ukraine was named Pinchas Tillman.

"What a coincidence," said the member, "He is my younger brother!" The older brother had left the Ukraine in 1910 during the

---

[25] "Kirya" is the Hebrew word for town.

[26] Incidentally, Golda Meir's kibbutz.

Second Aliyah. He knew Motl's parents, and he listened anxiously as Motl described the dramatic events that took place in the post-revolutionary period after 1917.

The next day, Motl travelled to Ein Harod, passing by Kibbutz Geva. When he arrived at Ein Harod he went directly to the office of the United Kibbutz Movement. He showed the Secretary his letter of introduction and explained that he had been advised to join the movement. After Motl described his experiences in *Eretz Yisrael*, the Secretary asked if Motl had a special place in mind. Motl answered that he would go wherever he was needed. He explained that for the next month and through the High Holy Days he planned to go from kibbutz to kibbutz until he arrived at Kfar Giladi, where his cousin Ada lived. The Secretary told Motl to go to Kfar Giladi and stay there until he received a letter telling him where he would be placed. He cautioned Motl to be more careful while traveling, as he would be leaving the Jezreel Valley and the protection of its many Jewish settlements. He also advised Motl to take the train to Kibbutz Gesher and seek out a couple named Davidka and Dvora who would show him their cooperative and tell him how to get from there to Kfar Giladi. Motl did not anticipate that he would eventually end up staying in Gesher.

He went to Gesher, where he was shown around by Dvora and Davidka, who also told him how to get to Kfar Giladi. First, he walked through the Jordan Valley to Degania, the oldest kibbutz in Palestine, which later split into two separate settlements, and then to the city of Tiberius, on a hill overlooking the Sea of Gallilee. There, he joined a group of *chalutzim* who were planning to settle in Kfar Giladi. They arranged a lift for Motl so that he arrived at Kfar Giladi just before the High Holy Days.

Motl was relieved to be at Kfar Giladi. He knew that this would be the last stop before his final destination. His cousin Ada, who was his mother's sister's youngest daughter, came to Palestine in 1924 with her boyfriend, Yonah, directly from Russia. Yonah became a jack-of-all-trades while Ada was a nurse, the same occupation that she'd had in Russia. Motl lived with them for a month while earning his keep as a volunteer worker. This gave him an opportunity to learn more about kibbutz life. He had much in common with Ada, who reminded him of his mother in looks and character. Ada wanted Motl to learn as much as possible about kibbutz life, so she gave him a book in Hebrew about the early years of Kfar Giladi, which was written by Ever Adeni, a member of the kibbutz. It was the first modern Hebrew book Motl had ever read, and while it was a difficult task he managed to get through it. He in turn gave Ada his khaki raincoat. As they were about the same size, it fit her perfectly.

Eliezer was one of the interesting personalities Motl met while staying with Ada. Eliezer was a large bearded man who was one of the legendary *Shomrim* (guards) that protected the *Yishuv*, the Jewish population of Palestine, during the *pre-Hagana* days from 1905 to 1929. When Eliezer asked if he could ride a horse, Motl told him about his experiences in western Canada. Motl then agreed to deliver some messages to the nearby settlement of Metulla on horseback. This gave Motl a chance to visit another cousin, Chana, his uncle Schmuel's youngest daughter. She had married a private farmer from Metulla. At Metulla, Motl discovered the two faces of *Eretz Yisrael*. Both Kfar Giladi and Metulla were sponsored by PICA (the Palestine Colonization Society) established by Baron Rothschild. However, while the members of Kfar Giladi showed economic initiative and ideological enthusiasm, the older, privately run farming settlements like Metulla remained old-fashioned, much like the small shtetls of Eastern Europe. They even continued to speak Yiddish. Wheat was their only crop. The farmers knew that if there was insufficient rain, PICA would carry the loss.

Metulla consisted of thirty-five families living without modern conveniences or appliances. They remained in this state until the establishment of the State of Israel, in 1948, when the Rothschild holdings were taken over by the government. While in the vicinity of Metulla, Motl also took the opportunity to visit a quarry and the Tanur,[27] a well-known waterfall that was one of the sources of the

---

[27] Hebrew for "oven".

Jordan River. He could see Mount Hermon and the mountains of Naftali in the distance.

During the month that he lived and worked in Kfar Giladi, Motl had time to think of his home in Montreal. Chienke kept in touch by mail. He learned that she had completed a second summer of work at Unzer Camp, and that she had organized a group of young idealists from Montreal and various other cities that planned to make *aliyah* during the summer of 1933. She wrote that Motl's family was surprised that he still hadn't found a permanent place to settle.

Motl tried to understand the various concerns that affected kibbutz life at that time. He attended public meetings and heard that one problem was that there were still only 200,000 Jews in the whole country! The swamps of the Hula Valley were still not drained and Kfar Giladi and Metulla were the only Jewish settlements north of Rosh Pinna. The settlers dreamt of a time when the swamps would be drained and there would be 500,000 Jews in Palestine.

One day the chairman of the Zionist Congress visited Kfar Giladi and addressed the community. The political situation was very gloomy. Lord Passfield, the British foreign minister, had tried to renege on the promise made by the Balfour Declaration. The Passfield White Paper restricted Jewish immigration to Palestine. The speaker tried to encourage his audience by ending with the Hebrew expression for, "Yihyeh Tov, Everything will be all right." When someone asked if he was certain it would be fine he answered in Yiddish that, "while there is no certainty there is hope."

During his stay at Kfar Giladi Motl also attended a shepherd's convention. The speakers emphasized the economic importance of sheep herding, that it had been an occupation of their forefathers, and that it should be modernized. A feast was prepared at the end of the session. A former yeshiva student performed a ritual slaughter of a sheep, but when he was done he was very pale; it's hard to find a Jew who is a tough guy! The meat was broiled on a bonfire and while Motl didn't want any at first, his appetite eventually got the better of him.

Part 3: Kibbutz Gesher

At last a letter arrived for Motl from kibbutz headquarters, directing him to Kibbutz Gesher. Motl accepted this directive with hope and goodwill. He wondered if Gesher would be suitable for Chienke and the others who might arrive with her. Motl said farewell to Ada and Yonah and the rest of Kfar Giladi and made his way to Gesher at the first opportunity.

When he arrived at Gesher, Motl went directly to the kibbutz secretary and presented the letter he had received from kibbutz headquarters and the letter of introduction from the Secretary of the Histadrut. The secretary, a dreamy type 35 to 40 years old, asked Motl to go to the wheat room to help sort and load the wheat into sacks. Motl was anxious to prove his worth as a worker. He worked by himself until another *chaver* came by and told him that from now on his name would be the Hebrew one, Mordechai. Since there was another Mordechai there already, Motl would be called Mordechai Hacanadi (Mordechai the Canadian). The same individual tested Mordechai's common sense by asking him to move the 100-kilo sacks of wheat to the upper level of the wheat room. When Mordechai asked for a wheelbarrow, the man smiled and said that he could see that Motl wasn't born in Canada. Nevertheless, Mordechai Hacanadi's motives remained suspect. Otherwise why would he leave prosperous Canada for Eretz Yisrael?

That evening, another smart aleck told Mordechai that he would have to sleep in the Arab village because the kibbutz had a space shortage. Mordechai wasn't pleased to hear this. He wanted to be with the other settlers and learn more about the operation of the kibbutz. Frieda, one of the older girls, noticed his reaction and mentioned that her hut had four beds but that only three girls were living in it. Why not place Mordechai with them? And so for the first few months, Mordechai stayed with three women who treated him like a younger brother. He learned about Gesher and its problems from them. Whenever they changed their clothes they asked him to close his eyes. And when he did as they asked they teased him for listening to them.

Frieda had a problem. When her family immigrated to America from Europe she had refused to go along. Instead, she made her way to Palestine. Now her family was urging her to come to America to visit them. Mordechai, and later Chienke, advised her to ask the Kibbutz for a leave of absence for one year. This would give her an opportunity to see America for herself and make a proper decision about her future. This is in fact what Frieda did. Many in the kibbutz were certain that she would not come back. But after a year, she did come back, for good.

Because he lived in a hut with women, Mordechai's first job placement was in the kitchen. After a while, however, he began to resent this. When one of his roommates mentioned this to the right party, Mordechai was placed in field work with a tractor team. His quarters were also changed. He now lived with five other young men in an old Arab house, built with lime and stone, once part of the now abandoned village of Gisser al Majana.

One of Mordechai's new roommates was Schmuel, brother of the dreamy kibbutz secretary who met Mordechai when he first arrived, and one of its leading personalities. He was one of the original group that had came to Gesher from Riga, Latvia. Schmuel was a sick man who couldn't do hard work. As he was an educated man, his job was to teach Hebrew to newcomers such as Mordechai. The other four roommates included Zeevi, also from Riga, whom Mordechai found to be a difficult person during his five years in Gesher, and Chaim, another of the group from Riga, a cynical and non-productive type whose main talent was writing feuilletons for the Kibbutz newsletter. There was also Chaim from South Africa, a tall attractive boy who received a lot of attention from the girls. Within a year, this Chaim would leave the Kibbutz for an American girl who fell in love with him when he was on a visit to Tel Aviv. The fifth roommate was Yosef, a newcomer from Cleveland. Yosef was a doctor of chemistry who came from an assimilated Russian-Jewish family that originated in Odessa. Yosef was well-educated and could speak English, Hebrew and Russian. His education was useless during the economic crisis of the 1930s, so he became a *chalutz*. Unfortunately, Yosef could not get adjusted to kibbutz life and within a year his parents brought him back home.

Although Mordechai had experience as a truck driver, he was assigned as a tractor helper for the midnight shift. The tract of land worked by this shift, in an area called the Bagara, belonged to the electric company and was located on the other side of the Jordan River. To get there, Mordechai had to walk three kilometres into Trans-Jordan along a dirt road used by Bedouins and their camel caravans. Needless-to-say, Mordechai was afraid, but he didn't want the others to think he was a coward. He arrived at the field shortly after it had rained. The previous shift's helper told him that the tractor wouldn't start and left him alone to wait for the mechanics. While waiting, Mordechai unscrewed the spark plugs, wiped them dry and replaced them. The tractor started when he turned the crank. Next, Mordechai lit the lanterns, sat on the tractor and began ploughing. The mechanics could see the tractor moving from a distance. Their first thought was that Arab marauders must have killed Mordechai and were now making off with the equipement. When they were nearer and saw that it was Mordechai, they became angry and asked him how he could dare to work by himself. In reply, Mordechai asked how they could dare to send him to this remote location by himself. The mechanics smiled and said that someone from the kibbutz had been watching to see that he was okay.This was yet another test for Mordechai Hacanadi.

The seeding and ploughing was done in fields of the Bagara and Dalhamia, tracts of land in the Jordan Valley near the Sea of Galilee. The land belonged to the Palestine Colonization Association (PICA) and was located in the general area where Kibbutz Degania was located and where Kibbutz Gesher was eventually supposed to be built. Unfortunately, the rains did not arrive on time and the entire crop was lost. Mordechai began to understand the complexities involved in establishing a kibbutz.

Part 4: The Establishment of Kibbutz Gesher

The settlement was originally established by PICA in 1925, under Baron Edmund Rothschild. The Baron paid little direct attention to his holdings, and the administrators he installed were not Zionists.

They looked upon the settlers as charity cases needing handouts, and it was not in their interest to encourage innovation and initiative. They certainly had no sympathy or interest in the cooperative ideals of the kibbutz movement.

It happened that during World War I, when communication between Paris and Palestine was difficult, the local PICA administrator, a man named Kalevinsky, who sympathized with the chalutzim, permitted the establishment of cooperative settlements for the Jewish guards (the *shomrim*, the parmilitary force that pre-dated the Hagana). This resulted in the formation of Kfar Giladi and Ayyelet Ha-Shahar, in the upper Gallilee. Another settlement was supposed to be established at Gisser-al-Majana, a plot of land by an old crusader bridge across the Jordan River at a waterfall where the river exits the Kinneret (the Sea of Galilee). The first Jewish settlers were the *Bashkirim*, immigrants from a remote Ural part of Russia.

The *Bashkirim* renovated the old stone and lime houses left behind by the Arab *fellahin* (farmers) who had inhabited the area in earlier times. Through PICA, a stone kitchen and dining room, a large wooden hut for a children's home, and a tin sheet bath house, partitioned for men and women, were built. Water for drinking and cooking was pumped directly from the Jordan River. Only a small portion of the land, a few hundred dunams next to the river, was suitable for intensive agriculture. The rest of the land was a hilly part of the Jordan Valley with uncertain rainfall that was useless to the settlers. The Bashkirim began to abandon the place.

In 1924 Pinhas Rutenberg, a Russian-born engineer contracted to build a hydroelectric plant at Naharayim, a point where the Yarmuk and Jordan Rivers join and drop 30 metres to the lower Jordan Valley. The Jewish settlement at Gisser-al-Majani was close to Naharayim, but by this time only one of the families of Bashkirim, the Kallmans, remained. The Jewish Agency arranged for a new group of immigrants, a group from Riga, Latvia, to settle there in order to provide a source of Jewish labour.

This group of *chalutzim* was comprised mainly of former students with secondary- or university-level education, or with yeshiva backgrounds. Most of them came from middle class Jewish homes. They came with Zionist and socialist convictions, and with the intention of building a modern collective in Palestine. When they approached PICA and the electric company for support it was not as beggars asking for charity. The electric company needed their labour, so they were hired and paid the standard wage. The matter of the establishment of a permanent settlement was left to PICA. However, the Baron's bureaucrats were not interested in the group's ideals. While they could not expel them, they refused to provide the funds needed to establish a permanent settlement.

That was the situation when Motl (Mordechai) arrived in 1932. The settlement, Gesher, was still a temporary one after 17 years. The hydroelectric project was almost complete and the settlers would be left with 3000 dunams[28] of marginally suitable wheat fields in Delhama as their only means of support. Because of the uncertain rainfall in this area they had even lost money in their efforts to grow a crop.

There were still no funds from PICA for a permanent settlement. The attitude of the electric company to the *chalutzim* was the same: The company needed them, but only as a labour force. It was not in the company's interest to help the *chalutzim* establish themselves as farmers. After all, farming might involve using large quantities of water from the Yarmuk River and this could reduce the flow of water to the turbines located downstream. So, during the winter of 1932-33 the group decided that it would have to rely on its own means to establish itself permanently. This would involve sending a group of chaverim to do outside work. Their earnings would be used to build a new settlement on the plot of land, Delhama, near the Yarmuk. Successful occupation of the land meant eventual ownership, in accordance with the old Turkish law still in effect. For a time there was work for the electric company. This involved building a bridge and a three metre high dam at the point where the Jordan River leaves

---

[28] A dunam is 1000 square metres.

the Kinneret. The dam was intended to raise the level of the Kinneret (Sea of Galilee) to provide a reserve supply of water during the summer.

Part 5: Motl (Mordechai) Establishes Himself at Kibbutz Gesher

When Mordechai, and later Chienke, came to Gesher they had to integrate themselves around the four main elements that made up the kibbutz. These were: the Kallman family, from the original group— the *Bashkirim*, the group from Riga, the *Volim*— a group from the Ukrainian part of Poland, and *Sabras*— Jews born in Palestine. Those from Riga were the most intelligent and dominant part of the kibbutz, putting their stamp on every aspect of daily life in Gesher. Although the kibbutz was still a temporary settlement, every effort was made to provide an orderly life for its members. Due to the work available with the electric company, the standards in food and hygiene were a little higher than those of other *kibbutzim*. Nevertheless, life was hard for everyone, including Mordechai and later Chienke.

After the failure of the harvest on the Delhama and Bagura plots of land, the kibbutz decided to build a lasting settlement at Delhama. They planned to construct permanent buildings, including roofs, and then claim possession of the land as permitted by law. But where would they get the money they needed for building? It happened that at this time the Solel Boneh, a construction cooperative of *the Histadrut*, was given a contract to build a road from Afula to Mount Tabor.

Thirty young men from Gesher, one of them Mordechai, volunteered to work on the road. The rest of the workers, 100 in all, came from Kibbutz Yagur and from a camp of young pioneers stationed near Mount Gilboa. The job, which took four months to complete, involved the use of primitive tools and a lot of manual labour. First, they leveled the roadbed with picks and shovels. Then they covered it with earth, large stones and then gravel mixed with sand. The various materials were brought to the roadbed in straw baskets, passed from hand to hand in a human chain. An older and experienced chaver, who had arrived in Palestine in the Second Aliyah[29] and who said he was Ben Gurion's friend, worked at spreading the new roadbed. He sang as he worked and his skill and enthusiasm were admired by the younger workers. The only machine was a steamroller, operated by a fez-wearing Arab, who used it to smooth the new road. The road was finally surfaced with asphalt after the layer of sand was added.

This was Mordechai's first experience as a road builder. He was fulfilling the key Labour Zionist ideal of "conquest of labour" (in Hebrew, *kibbush ha-avodah*). The workers camped in an abandoned children's village. Their food was prepared by women from the three *kibbutzim*. On Saturdays and during rainy periods they could relax and enjoy themselves. They made many excursions to the nearby *kibbutzim* and *moshavim*. This gave Mordechai and the others a good view of the Jezreel Valley as well as tasty Sabbath meals. On one rainy day they walked to the railway station in Afula. Suddenly, a car carrying Ben Gurion and his entourage passed. The car stopped and Ben Gurion got out to speak to the youngsters. He asked Mordechai where he was from and was very interested when Mordechai replied that he was from Canada, and that more young people from Canada and the United States (including his close friend, Chienke) would be arriving soon.

That evening there was a lot of singing and dancing in the camp. There was also serious discussion about the in-gathering of the exiles, whether there was enough room in the small territory of Palestine for all the Jews of the world, and what about the Arabs who lived there. They concluded that since the land could support millions of Jews in Biblical times, without the help of modern technology, why not in our times?

---

[29] The second aliyah refers to the second wave of modern Jewish immigration to Palestine that took place from 1904 until 1914.

A new development awaited the volunteers on their return to Gesher. The Iraq Petroleum Company decided to lay a pipeline to Haifa on the Mediterranean Sea through Transjordan and Palestine. Since the portion of the line that extended from the Jordan River to the sea was largely across land that belonged to the Jewish National Fund, the Jewish Agency demanded that this part of the project should be handled by Jewish workers.

The same 100 young men were assigned the pipeline job, starting from Gesher. First, straight lengths of 12-inch diameter steel pipe, each length 30 meters (about 90 feet) long, were assembled in the fields of Gesher. The lengths were to be joined and laid in a ditch that was being prepared for that purpose. Mordechai and his friend Gershon wondered how the straight pieces of steel pipe would conform to the varying elevations of the land. They decided to cross the Jordan (illegally) to see how it had been done on the other side. Mordechai, who could of course speak English, explained their dilemma to the British engineers, who were happy to oblige. They showed them how long stretches of the pipe, even if it was made up of individual pieces of straight lengths, would bend like rubber when the cranes threw it into the ditch.

After this experience, Mordechai stayed in Gesher for a while. He knew that Chienke and her group of new chalutzim would be arriving soon. Mordechai was too shy to ask for time off to meet Chienke on her arrival in Tel Aviv. Instead, he asked the kibbutz secretary for permission to travel to Tel Aviv to meet Chienke and the group, to see if they would be interested in settling at Gesher. The secretary replied that he knew about the group from Canada and the United States, but that they had been influenced to go to Degania where there was a shortage of workers. So Mordechai lost his excuse for the trip to Tel Aviv.

When Mordechai finally met Chienke after she had arrived at Degania, she demanded an apology. Mordechai explained that he didn't want to separate her from her group as soon as they had arrived in *Eretz Yisrael*. They needed her for her knowledge of Hebrew and pioneering life. Chienke accepted this explanation and offered

Mordechai an apple from the basket of fruit she had been given in New York.

Their romance continued from where it had left off. During the next six months Mordechai visited Degania often. At times Mordechai took Chienke for romantic evenings on the Kinneret using a rowboat he borrowed from fishermen he knew. They discussed the question of whether Mordechai should join Chienke at Degania, which was an established kibbutz. Mordechai argued that he would prefer to remain at Gesher because of the challenge of being a part of a new development.

Meanwhile, Mordechai and the group of kibbutz workers were sent to Migdal Tzedek on a new assignment. The year was 1933, the year that Hitler came to power in Germany. At this point in time, German Jews were allowed to leave Germany with some of their assets. Many came to Palestine, thereby creating a building boom. While the chalutzim had shown that they could be excellent builders, the building materials, mainly stone and sand, were supplied only by Arabs. As a result, the Histadrut and the Jewish National Fund began to acquire land in more mountainous regions of the country, in order to develop modern quarries for the building trade. One quarry was being established at Migdal Tzedek in the mountains of Ephraim, near the town of Petach Tikva. The same 100 workers were given the challenge of making another breakthrough in *kibbush ha-avodah*. Thus, for some months Chienke and Mordechai were separated again, except for Mordechai's Saturday visits. They decided to make a decision on whether to settle in Degania or Gesher at the end of the Migdal Tzedek project.

The workers set up camp at Kibbutz Givat Hasheloshah. This meant that they had a two-hour walk (12 kilometres) from camp to work. They worked in two shifts of nine hours each, with an hour for lunch. Sometimes they could get a ride back to camp on a loaded truck. When they demanded transportation to and from work, the manager cried out, "What kind of chalutzim are you?"

Mordechai worked very hard, but he also had some interesting experiences. The volunteers lived in tents, but ate and enjoyed their leisure hours with the rest of the kibbutz. One evening, Dr. Yehuda Kaufmann (later, Even Shmuel), another former Montrealer and well-known Hebrew writer, gave a lecture. From him Mordechai learned that Chaim Greenberg, leader of the *Poale Zion* and philosopher/editor of the *Yiddisher* Kemfer newspaper, would be speaking at an *Oneg Shabbat* at the Tel Aviv cultural hall on the next Saturday. These weekly events were initiated by the renowned Hebrew poet, Chaim Nahman Bialik, and were continued after his death by Dr. Kaufmann.

Mordechai didn't want to lose such an opportunity. He convinced his *chaverim* from Gesher to make a pilgrimage to Tel Aviv with him. That Saturday, they left right after breakfast to walk to the cultural hall, eating lunch along the way. By the time they arrived at 2 p.m. they were very tired. Mordechai and his friends were a little noisy when they entered the hall, and Dr. Kaufman didn't approve. However, when Mordechai explained that they had walked 12 kilometres, all was forgiven. It turned out that Menachem, the Muktar (headman) of Gesher, was also there. Mordechai and his fellow chaverim were treated to a meal in a restaurant and to a theatrical play about the biblical story of Jacob and Rachel. In order to better portray the biblical period, the actors had spent some time living with a Bedouin tribe. At the end of the day, Menachem paid for a shared taxi (a *sherut*) to take his tired *chaverim* back to camp.

The young Jewish volunteers worked at the quarry along with some Arab workers. The Jewish workers ate lunch together, sharing a big pot of tea and a food parcel provided by the communal kitchen of Kibbutz Givat Hashlosha. The Arab workers prepared and ate their food individually. Each had a supply of flour, water, oil and spices along with a large round-bottomed bowl. First, they built a fire with dried grass and heated the bowls. After mixing the dough with their hands they flattened it into a pita and baked it, one side at a time, on the bottom of the bowl. After adding oil and spices it was ready to eat.

The group from Gesher included a few *chalutzim* from Damascus, who could speak fluent Arabic. They had a number of friendly conversations with the Arab workers, but when they tried to explain the kibbutz idea and way of life to the Arabs, they would hold up their hands after a while and say, "enough".

During this period of work at the quarry, Mordechai also had the opportunity to participate in the election of representatives to the Zionist Congress. Naturally, the kibbutz membership supported Labour. The volunteer workers voted at their camp in Givat Hashlosha before going to work in the morning. The same evening Sonia, a chavera[30] from Montreal, visited Mordechai and asked him to escort her to an election meeting, where Chaim Greenberg was giving an address. Greenberg contrasted the Labour Zionists with their right wing rivals, the Revisionists, by comparing the latter to the Hungarian hangman who worked at a jail in Vienna, Austria. When Hungary was liberated after the First World War, he decided to return to his homeland. "Why should I continue to hang people in Vienna when I can hang people in my own country?" In other words, fascists are fascists, whether or not from your own people.

The next Saturday, Mordechai attended a celebration by the Mapai wing of the Labour party in Tel Aviv. The highpoint in Mordechai's memory was a speech by Yosef Sprinzak, a leading *chaver*, who became the first speaker of the *Knesset* after the establishment of the State of Israel. At this point, Chaim Weizmann had been temporarily ousted and replaced by Nahum Sokolow as president of the World Zionist Congress. Sprinzak appealed to the audience, reminding them that Weizmann was the only Zionist leader with an international reputation, and that the movement could not continue without him. In fact, Weizmann was returned to office at the next Congress.

At last PICA agreed to support Gesher's efforts to establish a permanent settlement at Delhama and the workers at the quarry were called home. Mordechai began to visit Chienke at Degania more often. The older *chaverim* at Degania loved Chienke for her devotion to *chalutziut* and for her wonderful sense of humour. But they worried about Mordechai walking back and forth alone so they advised Chienke to join Mordechai at Gesher. And that is what happened.

---

[30] In Hebrew, female for friend.

Chienke impressed the *chaverim* at Gesher. They saw a role for her in child development, and that is the area she worked in during her four years at Gesher.

Chienke and Mordechai still had to make their decision official. On the first Friday that they were together, Mordechai got up the courage to ask the kibbutz Secretary for an English half pound, the amount charged to the *chalutzim* by the rabbi in Moshava Kinneret for a traditional Jewish wedding, complete with certificate. Mordechai was too shy to specify what the money was for, but the Secretary already knew. So the groom, Mordechai, wearing his khaki shorts and light blue shirt, and the bride, Chienke, wearing a blue skirt and white blouse, walked to Kinneret. First, they stopped at Degania to see if someone would be their witness and to borrow a ring from their friend Tzipora. Ezra, a *chaver* who wasn't working, came along to be the witness. When the rabbi asked Mordechai where the ring was from, Mordechai answered that it was a borrowed ring. The rabbi replied that a borrowed ring could not be used. He asked Mordechai if he had a silver coin. Mordechai gave him a shilling. With the coin he performed the wedding rites, in accordance with *halacha* (Jewish religious law).

The three of them, Chienke, Mordechai and the witness, went to the Arab village of Zemah, where they bought frozen sodas, which they used to drink a *l'chaim*. Then the newlyweds walked back to Gesher. It was sunset when they arrived. On entering the dining hall they were amazed to see a sign on the wall saying, "*Mazel Tov* to Chienke and Mordechai." After supper and a group sing-song, Chienke and Mordechai were told that the only housing available for the two of them was a tent. And that is how they began their life together.

After a short honeymoon of a few days, Mordechai was assigned to night guard duty for a week. Two weeks later Chienke was assigned to night duty at the children's home. In the meantime, the problem of building a permanent settlement in Delhama became acute. The main difficulty was in finding qualified builders. The hiring of outside labourers, even Jewish ones, was unthinkable. Solel Boneh, the *Histadrut* construction company, suggested that the kibbutz send a group of 30 to 40 young men to work on a large apartment building that was under construction in the name of David Hacohen, a prominent member of *Histadrut*, the General Federation of Labour, and later Israeli politician, in the Hadar neighbourhood of Haifa. By working with qualified tradesmen, the men would obtain the experience needed by the kibbutz.

Mordechai was one of the candidates considered for work in Haifa. But how could he be separated from Chienke, his new bride? The kibbutz Secretary had a solution: Chienke would be sent to Haifa too, to prepare food for the construction workers. The hut for the workers consisted of one large dormitory for the men, a kitchen and dining room, and two small rooms, one for Chienke and Mordechai and one for two girls who worked in the kitchen with Chienke. At first, Chienke was concerned that she didn't have experience cooking for large groups, but the Secretary told her that she would learn from the two other girls. Besides, Chienke would have to also help maintain the kibbutz spirit and unity of the group. And that is how it worked out.

Construction work involves a number of different trades and skills. Mordechai was assigned to the department of wrought iron design along with three other members of the kibbutz: Moishe, the son of a blacksmith; Zeevi, a veteran kibbutznik; and Reuven, a newcomer from Germany who had studied electronics. The tradesman who was supposed to teach them used to have a snack in the dining room. One day as he was chatting with Chienke, he mentioned that the four young men from the kibbutz were having trouble grasping his trade. When Chienke mentioned that one of them was her Mordechai, the man said, "He is so quiet and shy." Chienke replied, "even still water penetrates iron."

The tradesman paid more attention to Mordechai. It happened that Moishe never attended a technical school and could not read a blueprint. Zeevi, the oldtimer who had, he said, completed high school in Russia, liked to command and shout orders but couldn't get along with the others. Reuven, who had received technical training in Germany, could not deal with the practical decisions of coordinating workers and materials. In time, the tradesman found that Mordechai had all of the qualities needed for the trade.

Eventually, when the group returned to Gesher, Mordechai became one of a trio involved in building the new settlement in Delhamma. There was David, one of the Latvians, another David, of the Voliners, and Mordechai, Hacanadi. Mordechai was in charge of coordination; that is, reading the blueprints and scheduling the order of the work.

During the day, Mordechai and Chienke were apart, he in Delhama while she worked in the children's home in Gesher. At this time, Chienke became pregnant. Mordechai reflected on his three years at Gesher and realized that he still didn't feel completely integrated into the kibbutz. He tried hard to make up for it in his own way but it was not easy. Chienke experienced the same difficulty, but it seemed to Mordechai that she was more accepted. Mordechai felt that the different factions that formed the provisional settlement of Gesher were able to deal with matters pertaining to order and cleanliness and cultural activities. But when it came to the building of a permanent home, the common sense of purpose disappeared and the different factions began to fight for position. Although Chienke and Mordechai were highly respected, they didn't have many close friends.

One day, after a number of months, Chienke began to experience birth pains. While she was in Gesher Mordechai was working in Delhama. The kibbutz doctor ordered her to leave for the hospital in Afula right away. A few hours later, someone told Mordechai that he was the father of a baby boy. After receiving the congratulations of those around him, Mordechai was jokingly asked by one of the older *chaverim* if he appreciated the responsibility of fatherhood. When Mordechai arrived at the hospital, Chienke showed him a beautiful little girl. She asked Mordechai if he would mind if they called her Miriam, after her mother. Of course Mordechai agreed. It turned out that the message that was sent to the kibbutz started as, "To Mordechai Ben (son of) David" and this was accidentally shortened to,"To Mordechai ben (a son)."

When Chienke became pregnant, she and Mordechai were assigned to living quarters in a wooden hut with a partition. Sara, the hut's other occupant, was a highly educated Jerusalemite with extravagant tastes. Sara was involved in education, and worked with Chienke in the kibbutz. This, and her interest in learning English, made her very close to Chienke and Mordechai. In fact, Sara was married and had a child. But she and her husband, an uneducated playboy type who worked as a mechanic in Gesher, were separated. After the move to a permanent site in Delhama, to what later became known as Kibbutz Ashdot Yaacov, Sara, an old-timer, was entitled to one of the new concrete block apartments. Instead, she insisted on continuing to share a hut with Chienke and Mordechai.

In spite of the friendships they had made, Chienke and Mordechai and their daughter Miriam did not feel fully integrated into the kibbutz. Gesher was composed of too many different factions. The group from Riga maneuvered between the various elements in order to maintain their dominant position. They included Mordechai and Chienke in their circle when they were needed and pushed them away when they were not.

While there were difficulties, Mordechai, Chienke and Miriam had a good life in the kibbutz. Mordechai continued to work in construction, while Chienke was involved in the important task of looking after the children's home. This was the period of youth aliyah from Germany. Mordechai was asked to assist in integrating the new arrivals into the kibbutz work force. He found it difficult to communicate with them in Yiddish until he met a young blond girl, Irena, who spoke fluent English. Irena, the daughter of a banker from Dusseldorf, had completed her aliyah training in Luxemburg. She told Mordechai that she was used to hard work, and asked that she be given a man's job. Irena became Mordechai's first assistant in wrought iron construction. Because of her university background and knowledge of mathematics they became an excellent team.

Mordechai and Irena became friends. As they worked, they described their experiences to each other. Some of the members of the kibbutz thought that they were becoming too friendly, especially as Mordechai was a family man. In spite of Irena's protests, the committee that dealt with family matters moved her to new job as a night guard at the children's home. When Chienke came around to check up on the new guard, Irena told her that there were no romantic intentions between her and Mordechai. In fact, she had a serious boyfriend from her days in training in Luxemburg. Chienke went to the committee and in her good-natured way told them that she was not worried. Jokingly she told them that she wasn't going to get lucky enough to lose Mordechai and that Irena should be allowed to continue to work in construction. And that's the way it was for two years.

Life in the kibbutz didn't revolve solely around work and political intrigue. The hut that housed the library was the most popular part of the kibbutz. A learned member of the kibbutz, another Mordechai, was in charge of it. However, this Mordechai lacked organizational ability. Many of the books, journals and newspapers were misplaced, while the hut itself was left untidy. Mordechai and Irena were nominated by the cultural committee to do something about it. They went around the kibbutz collecting various items and placing them in proper order in the library. Saturdays were spent cleaning and tidying the library with the assistance of some of the other newcomers from Germany.

One night of the week was devoted to classical music. Due to the lack of electricity, the kibbutz had to make do with an old-fashioned wind-up phonograph. But the records that they listened to were the best, and Dvora, the musical expert, explained the significance of each piece. Thanks to this experience Mordechai and others like him learned to appreciate good music for the rest of their lives.

About one half of the five years that Mordechai spent at Gesher involved various work missions outside the kibbutz. The rest of his workdays were in construction projects in Delhama. Evenings were spent with Chienke and Miriam (Mirale). Miriam was an exceptionally smart and attractive child who brought much joy and family strength to Chienke and Mordechai. Just as Chienke was not lucky to be rid of him, so Mordechai was lucky that Chienke worked mainly with women. The doctor was the only male that she had anything to do with, and although he had proclaimed that Chienke was the finest and most attractive woman in Gesher, Mordechai didn't worry about him.

The social life of Gesher started with a sing-song and *Oneg Shabbat* (literally, joy of Sabbath) stroll with family and friends after the Friday evening meal. Various committees met on Saturday mornings after a Sabbath breakfast. Since Chienke was busy with matters related to the children's home, it was Mordechai's duty to look after Mirale. Since he didn't have a carriage, he carried her on his shoulder as he walked through the orange and grapefruit groves. Saturday afternoons were for naps and reading and family discussions, until sunset. Then it was time for walks and outings by married couples as well as by single men and women, and by youngsters from *Youth Aliyah*. Some walked to the nearby railway station and others to the fruit groves. After supper, it was the custom to hold a general meeting. Any *chaver* could be present and take part in the discussions, but not everyone could vote.

The year 1934 was the tenth anniversary of Gesher's existence, and a special celebration was planned. Since the work in Delhama had already begun, and the celebration would be held in Gesher, there was the problem of deciding who would remain on guard in Delhama. One older chaver stated that the celebration was really for the veterans of Gesher, whereas the newest members were strangers and they should be the ones to remain on guard duty. This view upset Mordechai who raised his hand at a meeting and pointed out that the newest members were not strangers, that they had volunteered to come to the kibbutz, and that they were most important for its future success. Clearly, it was the duty of the older members to remain on guard duty in Delhamma. To Mordechai's amazement, his opinion was accepted unanimously.

The anniversary was held in the open air in an amphitheatre, in which the seats and stage were made from bales of straw. There were greetings and words of praise from various leaders of the kibbutz movement. The most important address was given by the head of the *Kibbutz ha-Meuchad* organization. He explained how a community was like a symphony with individuals of varying talents representing the different instruments that together produce great music.

Once the celebration was over it was time to pay attention to the widespread hostilities initiated by the Arabs throughout Palestine. Gesher was defenseless. There wasn't even a wire fence around the settlement. One day the Secretary came to the work site where Mordechai and his helpers were preparing the wrought iron used in construction. He asked that tiny pieces of iron be cut. No explanation was given and Mordechai didn't ask for one.

At this point, Mordechai still worked in Delhama during the day, returning to Gesher in the evening. One night the Arabs launched a surprise attack on Gesher. Mordechai and the rest of the *chaverim* rushed to the hastily built trenches. Ammunition was scarce but some of the chaverim had home-made hand grenades made with tiny bits of iron-from Mordechai's construction site. Those who knew how to use them threw them at the invaders, who became frightened and fled, taking their killed and wounded with them.

After this episode, the children and most of the *chaverim*, including Chienke and Mordechai, moved to the newly built Delhama location. Unfortunately, the friendly cultured lifestyle that existed in the provisional settlement of Gesher became lost when the kibbutz moved to Delhama. The question is, why? First, the effort to build a new settlement became the main focus of activity. Second, as already mentioned, Gesher was composed of rival factions. The newest group from Germany was a powerful one because the Jewish Agency allocated substantial funds for their absorption and because they were well educated and possessed a high level of technical knowledge. The other groups, including the one from Riga, were afraid of them. Individuals like Mordechai and Chienke suffered from all sides because they didn't belong to any of the main groups.

The recent Arab hostilities were another factor. Since the attacks often took place at around midnight, it was necessary to guard the kibbutz day and night. Everyone was involved in guard duty, some at night. Mordechai was excused from night duty because he worked all day and had important construction responsibilities. But Mordechai was offended by this special treatment and complained to his associate Davidka, who also commanded the defenders. Davidka obliged by giving him guard duty at night.

Mordechai and Chienke tried to relax in their apartment after supper while waiting for their night assignments. Mordechai was entrusted with a key to the ammunition cache hidden beneath the floor of the barn. Chienke was responsible for guarding the children's home. One attack began surprisingly early. Shots were fired, and Davidka could be heard ordering everyone to their positions. Mordechai ran to the ammunition cache and Chienke to the children's home. This time the raiders were scared off by a few shots before reaching the kibbutz.

Under these circumstances, Mordechai became physically drained and the doctor ordered him to go to Safed for a month of recuperation along with other *chaverim*. The rest gave him a chance to spend some time in the centre of Jewish mysticism. Along with the medieval cemetery and the old narrow streets, there was a modern Safed on Mount Canaan. Mordechai also had discussions about the problems of kibbutz life with the other *chaverim*. They concluded jokingly that everyone in a kibbutz should be alike. Unfortunately, some want to be more alike than the others!

When he returned to Delhama, Mordechai tried to get back into the old routine, but the political situation in the kibbutz had become more strained. The pressure on the Riga group by the German newcomers had increased. The Riga group tried to hold on to its dominant position with the help of the other factions. Chienke and Mordechai were caught in the middle.

One day, David of the Riga faction told Mordechai that from now on he should pass his construction quotations over to Zeevi, another old-timer from Riga, who would in turn hand them over to the building committee. Mordechai objected. "Why," he asked "shouldn't I continue to deal directly with the committee, as in the past?" David replied that it was necessary to enhance Zeevi's position in the kibbutz.

Mordechai was shocked by these developments. He was afraid to tell Chienke. He felt that she was well-established in the kibbutz, and he did not want to disturb her peace of mind. However, it turned out that Zeevi and his German-born wife, Judith, lived next door to Chienke and Mordechai. Zeevi began to knock on the thin wall separating them, asking Mordechai, "How much iron do we need and what lengths should we use?" and so on.

When Chienke heard this she asked what was going on, and Mordechai told her the whole story. Then Chienke said that she had a similar story to tell. Although she was well respected for her work with children, her co-workers had become jealous. They did whatever they could to belittle her. When the doctor came to check on the children's health they locked her out to keep the information away from her. In other words, as Chienke put it, her life in the kibbutz wasn't a bed of roses.

Part 6: Motl and Chienke Decide to Leave Gesher

At this point, Mordechai and Chienke decided that they had to leave Gesher, although not necessarily kibbutz life. But which kibbutz should they go to? Chienke hesitated to go back to Degania. There was a group of *Hashomer Hatzair* members, including Chienke's sister, Rochke, that Mordechai and Chienke could join in Hadera. However, to Mordechai and Chienke this would be same as capitulating and returning to an ideology they had left. So they decided to try private life in Haifa for a while. Perhaps they would find other newcomers from Canada who would be willing to form a moshav, a type of collective settlement in which family life remains private.

Mordechai and Chienke went to see Benjamin, the new kibbutz Secretary, and told him of their decision. He was shocked, as he had thought that Mordechai and Chienke were well established in Gesher. When they told them the reason, he tried to convince them that the problem was a minor one. A number of *chaverim* urged them to reconsider. They promised to stay for another half year until replacements could be trained to do their work. And so they did.

A number of incidents helped strengthen their decision. On one dark night when Mordechai was on guard duty he noticed someone moving. When he asked, "Who goes there?" a shot rang out in his direction. Pincus, a newcomer from Germany, came running to

Mordechai to see if he was injured. Pincus claimed that he didn't know that the gun was loaded. But Mordechai felt that he was really trying to scare him so that he would not reverse his decision. Pincus wanted to take over Mordechai's position once he left. In fact, that is what happened. Pincus eventually displaced the two Davids, and they also left the kibbutz.

After half a year, in late 1937, Mordechai, Chienke and Mirale (one and one-half years old) left Gesher with only the clothes that they wore, a pillow each, a pair of sheets and blankets and 10 English pounds (the equivalent, then, to fifty dollars). They were also given a letter of reference from the secretary stating that Mordechai and Chienke had worked and contributed to the fullest extent possible to the kibbutz.

In fact the concept of *chalutziut* and the ideal of kibbutz life never left Mordechai and Chienke, neither in their individual lives nor in their work. They kept their pioneering spirit alive during the year they spent in Haifa, and even when they returned to Montreal for what they thought would be a visit. The same spirit kept Mordechai going while he worked as a superintendent in the Adath Israel Congregation and later as an installment merchant. Chienke maintained her involvement through the Pioneer Women (Naamat) Organization and Mordechai in the Farband Labour Zionist Alliance. They passed the pioneering spirit on to their children and grandchildren.

Jacob's Commentary

The title of this chapter refers to the more Hebrew biblical term, *Eretz Yisrael*, or "Land of Isreal". Palestine is the term coined by the Romans in about 135 AD (or the Common Era, CE) after the second revolt against Roman rule. The first revolt took place about 60 years earlier and ended with the fall of Massada. After crushing the second revolt, led by Bar Kochva, the Romans replaced the existing name of Judea for Palestina, to emphasize the eradication of Jewish sovereignity. Jerusalem was destroyed and its replacement was given the name Aelia Capitalina.

The name Palestina originated from the name of the ancient coastal peoples, known as the Philistines. Palestine was never an independent entity again, and during Arab and Ottoman Turk rule, the area was part of what was referred to as Greater Syria. The name Palestine was revived in the early 20th century when the territory was severed from the Ottoman Empire with the defeat of Turkey, toward the end of World War I. Ottoman rule was replaced by a British Mandate under the auspices of the League of Nations. The term "Palestinian" referred to both Jews and Arabs, and during his time in Palestine my father considered himself to be a Palestinian. Indeed, the Jerusalem Post newspaper (the only English language daily in Israel) and the Israel Philharmonic Orchestra were originally called the Palestine Post and the Palestine Philharmonic, respectively. When the State of Israel was declared in 1948, its name was chosen from a range of possibilities, including Judea. Gradually over a number of years and to at least some extent by default, the term "Palestinian" began to be used to denote the Arab population of Palestine, and not the Jews.

This chapter also brings up what is to my mind one of the more fascinating aspects related to the Holocaust and to the formation of the State of Israel, and that is the immigration of German Jews to Palestine during the early period of Nazi government. In fact, between the years 1933 and 1936 an estimated 174,000 Jews immigrated to Palestine, mainly from Eastern Europe and Germany. This number represents almost a third of the total number of Jews in Palestine (600,000) at the time of the establishment of the State of Israel in 1948. In fact, as my father notes earlier in this chapter, the Jewish population of Palestine when he made *aliyah* was only about 200,000.

There were approximately 500,000 Jews in Germany when the Nazi party took power in 1933. Of these, about 300,000 managed to emigrate before the start of the Second World War, while the remainder, about 200,000, were deported and murdered in the years that followed. The destinations of those that emigrated included the United States, Great Britain, Latin America (especially South America), China (Shanghai) and Palestine. About 60,000 immigrated to Palestine, from 1933. Ultimately, rioting and civil unrest by the Arab population of Palestine, which led to a decrease of the number of Jews admitted by British Mandatory officials to Palestine, as well as the outbreak of World War II, ended this wave of immigration.

Another feature of this immigration is that it was undertaken as part of an agreement, the Transfer Agreement (or *Haarava*, in Hebrew) between the German Government and the Jewish Agency in Palestine, an agreement which was concluded in 1933. At this point, it is useful to note that the Jewish Agency was a quasi-governmental body that existed in Palestine before the establishment of the State of Israel, and one of its functions was the absorption of Jewish immigrants from the Diaspora. The Transfer Agreement made it possible for Jewish immigrants to take some of their wealth with them by allowing them to purchase German goods and export them to Palestine. The agreement was also designed to stall Jewish efforts to organize an economic boycott of Germany, a factor that made it highly controversial among Jewish leaders in the Diaspora.

The agreement made it possible for a substantial number of well-educated German Jewish businessmen and professionals to immigrate to Palestine along with some of their capital at a critical point in the history of the State of Israel, particularly with respect to its early industrial development. For example, Stef Wertheimer, the founder of ISCAR, one of the largest manufacturers of industrial cutting tools in the world, and a company in which the billionaire investor Warren Buffet purchased a controlling interest for 5 billion dollars in 2006, immigrated from Germany to Palestine in 1937.

This is a good point to bring up the term "Yekke," a mildly derogatory term used by people such as my parents to describe German Jews. It was used to describe someone who is excessively pedantic, or rule and schedule-oriented. It is a term I heard many times when I was a child, and I simply assumed that it was a Yiddish word. However, in thinking about it in recent years as I became more personally involved in these memoirs, I finally asked a colleague who speaks fluent German if he knew the meaning. He did, and it is derived from the German word for "jacket." Now I understood! The immigrants from Germany were used to a more formal lifestyle and dress, and I suppose the men wore sport or suit jackets. They must have stood out in the hot climate of Palestine.

Both Weizmann and Sokolow, who are mentioned in this chapter, were leading figures in world Zionist circles, and both had served as Congress presidents in the past. Sokolow was a prolific writer and pioneer of Hebrew journalism while Weizmann was a renowned scientist who made a major contribution to the British war effort during World War I. He later became the first president of the independent state of Israel. Both men lived in Britain during World War I and both were instrumental in encouraging the 1917 Balfour Declaration, which stated that the British Government viewed with favour the establishment in Palestine of a national home for the Jewish people. The 1931 World Zionist Congress was a fractious meeting, caused mainly by the perception of a weakening of British sympathy for Zionist activity following the Arab riots of 1929. Many of the delegates, particularly the more activist Revisionists, felt that Weizmann was too cooperative with the British. Sokolow, who was seen to be less of an anglophile than Weizmann, was elected president instead of Weizmann. Weizmann resumed the presidency in 1935 after the Revisionists withdrew from the World Zionist Congress.

My father enjoyed his job of preparing and cutting the rebar or rods used for reinforcing concrete. As related in this chapter, the job was part of the early development of Solel Boneh, a cooperative-based construction company, now a major construction conglomerate with projects in various parts of the globe. My father had no formal construction training but he was very good at mental arithmetic and had no trouble reading construction plans and figuring out the rebar needs for various projects. The salaries of the young kibbutz men doing the work were given to the central kibbutz budget. One of the major projects he worked on was the Rutenberg electrical generating plant on the Jordan River, where he witnessed the accidental electrocution of a co-worker. He was also involved in road and railroad construction, and he loved to tell me how the rails were bent to create a turn in the railroad. (You wait until you have a long stretch of say half a kilometre of interconnected straight rails, and then use iron spikes driven into the long end to gradually bend the rail in the desired direction. This is the same approach as that which he describes in relation to the construction of the Iraq-Haifa petroleum pipeline.)

My father and mother's time on the kibbutz came to an end indirectly as a result of the wave of German Jewish immigration to Palestine in the 1930s. On their kibbutz, the newcomers exacerbated the factional tensions that already existed. As a result, my father was expected to relay the information needed to prepare the rebar to another individual who would be given the credit for doing the job. This was something my father could not do, and so he and my mother and my sister left the kibbutz with just the clothes on their backs. As I grew up and listened to my parents' stories, I always had the impression that they regretted their decision to leave. Many years later, in 1978-79, I and my wife, Barbara, and our three young children, spent 10 months in Haifa where I was on a sabbatical leave. It turned out that my primary host was a scientist whose uncle was from Ashdod Yaakov, the current name of the kibbutz my parents left in 1937. When I mentioned this to my parents, who were visiting us in Israel at the time, along with the scientist's surname, my father remarked that this was the same individual who had caused them to leave!

I'll end my comments to this chapter on a lighter note in relation to a song my father mentions in the early part of the chapter. He sang it on a *Haganah* march, held in Haifa during his visit to his relatives in 1932. As he noted, the song refers to playing with the waves and becoming angels, and the march was held both as a show of strength to the Arab population and, since it was held on the Sabbath, to show disdain to Jewish orthodoxy. While writing these comments and reediting my father's words I tried to find out the meaning of the song. Unfortunately, my father is not here to tell me. Initially, I thought it might have had a liturgical or biblical source, perhaps from the story of Jonah, but none surfaced. I then consulted with Israeli friends, both here in Canada and in Israel and they in turn cast a broad net of inquiries. One possibility mentioned was that the song was from a poem by the well-known Israeli poet, Yehuda Amichai. However, Amichai was born in 1924 and my father was writing about events in 1932. Another possibility that came up was the lyrics were by a composer-song writer named Moshe Bick, who lived in Haifa and wrote songs about workers and pioneers. One song, about workers paving roads, was suggested as the source of my father's song. However, a closer look at the words indicated some overlap in wordage, such as the term "waves", but not enough to be convincing. Finally, the same friend sent a scanned copy of the actual song. It is in fact a well known but ribald street song about a young lady named Samara (or Tamara) looking for a good time on the beach with a sailor. Interestingly, the Hebrew words for "sailor" and "angel" are very similar. Perhaps my father didn't really understand what the song was about. After all, he heard it during the early part of his stay in Palestine, when his Hebrew was probably not very fluent. In fact, a quick internet search of the two words led me to a biblical study of Jonah, *Forgiveness in a Wounded World*, by Janet Howe Gaines, in which mention is made of the possible double meaning (sailor/angel, page 45) to an audience hearing an oral presentation.

Chapter 5: Leaving The Kibbutz

Part 1: Haifa

At first, Mordechai went to Haifa by himself. His relatives, the Gorodetsky family, were astonished to hear that Chienke and Mordechai had decided to leave Gesher. How could such idealists make such a decision, especially during very trying political and economic times? Mordechai tried to explain but they could not understand. In fact, they told him about a professor at the Technion-Israel Institute of Technology, who often shopped at their grocery store and who had been well off, but who had now decided to join Kibbutz Gesher because of the hard times. Go explain the problems of kibbutz life to middle-class people! The professor had good friends among the veteran Riga faction of the kibbutz. When the economy in Palestine worsened, he asked his friends in Gesher if he and his family could join. His friends felt so priviliged to be asked that they ignored the wishes of the other *chaverim*. They made sure that the professor and his family was accepted and that he was eligible for special privileges.

Mordechai didn't lose his bearings. He used his reference from the *Histadrut* Secretary to get a job in the iron construction trade. The Port of Haifa had been completed and a new business district (Hamelachim Street) was going up on the newly reclaimed land. Mordechai worked there for a month, and this enabled him to bring Chienke and Miriam to Haifa.

They rented a room with a tiny kitchenette in a cottage built on the slope of Mount Carmel. Four families lived in the cottage. The owner and his wife with two children lived in two rooms with a regular kitchen and a private bathroom. Chienke and Mordechai lived in the semi-basement with two other couples. They shared a shower and a toilet. In their own way, the owners were also pioneers. They all got along very well, especially with Mirale.

Although there were two other children in the house, a boy, Joshua, and a girl, Harella, Miriam managed to get most of the attention. She spoke fluent Hebrew and she was already a keen observer. Once when she was walking with Chienke and Mordechai on the street, she saw a woman wearing gloves. "Look" she said, "she's wearing socks on her hands." Joshua didn't get along with his own sister but he was always generous to Miriam. On one occasion when he was sick Miriam was told not to play with him because he was contagious. When he tried to convince her to play with him she said, "*Bukra fil mish-mish*", which is an Arabic saying meaning, "tomorrow there will be apricots," meaning, "like fun I will do it!" The owners of the cottage often invited her to join their meals. When she came into their house she said, in Hebrew, "Malka, where is my chair"?

Chienke became the generous hostess of the house. Her sister Rochke and her friend Malka often visited from their temporary kibbutz in Hadera. Malka had to leave the kibbutz to work in Haifa to help her mother, so she became a frequent visitor, as did Sheindel of Ramat Yochanan, whose husband Zalman had been killed in an accident. Sheindel and a number of girlfriends usually visited Friday evenings, often eating up the food that had been prepared for the Sabbath. Thank God Mirale was invited to eat with the owner's family. Chienke and Mordechai could usually count on an offer of cholent (a traditional Jewish stew that is simmered overnight before the Sabbath) when they visited the Gorodetskys. But one Saturday all they got was peanuts and cold water!

There were other visitors as well: Sheindel's mother, *chavers* Zuker, Schreiber and Dresher, and finally Chienke's sister Rivke, with her husband Isaac and their daughter Miriam. Rivke and her family were returning to Montreal after trying life in Palestine.

When the job near the Port of Haifa was completed, Mordechai's situation became more serious. At first he worked with another former Montrealer in a shop that sold floor tiles, but Mordechai could not work in a non-unionized setting. Then a bookkeeper friend who worked on the Carmel, a suburb of Haifa, tried get him work maintaining the municipal water tower. However, to get the job Mordechai needed the *protektzia* (influence) of a rabbi, a religious functionary, from the Mizrachi party. Nothing came of it, although Mordechai did get to see the rabbi's lavish lifestyle. Later, in Montreal, Mordechai met the same rabbi when he was on a fundraising trip. When he recognized Mordechai he quickly disappeared.

Finally, Mordechai got a job on a Solel Boneh (*Histadrut*) project involving the building of a dam to cool the turbines of the Haifa electricity plant. There were rumours that the project was part of an English plan to build a secret submarine base.

At first, the workers had to clear and level part of a stone mountain to a width of 50 metres and to a depth of one metre, by removing the wild vegetation and earth. Then they used compressors to drill holes about 10 metres down. These were filled with dynamite, which was ignited electrically using wires that extended from the rock face to the site office. The workers gathered in the office for safety. With a push of the ignitor button, one wall of the mountain collapsed, creating a pile of rubble that included rocks and stones of a variety of sizes. Now three groups of workers, five to a group, scrambled over the rocks with chains around their necks to look for the largest ones. These they bound with the chains so that the rocks could be pulled on to trucks. The work was an intellectual challenge as well as a physical one for if the chains were not placed properly the rocks could roll in the wrong direction, killing or injuring the workers or damaging the truck.

In the course of the work, Mordechai had to instruct the other four in his group how to choose the rocks to be moved and how to place the chains to pull them out of the pile. On more than one occasion, movement of one rock caused others in the pile to crumble and roll and the workers had to run for safety.

It was dangerous work. The workers had to rely on each other in order to survive. They warned each other when a stone or rock was falling so they could get out of the way. Often the one giving the warning lost valuable time for himself. Once when Mordechai was late coming home from work, Chienke called his workplace, using the only telephone in the neighbourhood. She was told that the work had been delayed for two hours. Chienke was the only wife who called. One of Mordechai's associates, a man from a small shtetl in Poland, was amazed that he had such an intelligent wife that she knew how to use the telephone!

One of Mordechai's co-workers, Moshe Avineri, was from a very orthodox background from Krakow, Poland. Moshe was originally a yeshiva student[31] who changed direction and became a member of the *Hashomer Hatzair*. Mordechai's initial impression was that he looked odd, in part because of his strange moustache. Moshe wanted to befriend Mordechai, so he told him his story.

Moshe arrived in Palestine in the late 1920s. He joined a temporary kibbutz in Nes Tziona, which later dissolved. At this point, Moshe became a private (bonded) worker. He was attracted to the ideals of the *Left Poale Zion*, particularly to the view that Arab and Jewish workers had to work together to create a state in Palestine. To get closer to the Arabs, the former yeshiva student learned to speak Arabic and visited Arab cafes. The British secret police did not mind when Jews became involved in socialism or even communism, but they were not prepared to allow such ideas to spread among the Arabs. When Moshe was caught agitating he was arrested and expelled from Palestine without trial, even though it was illegal to expel a Jew from his homeland. The political secretary of the Zionist Agency, Arlosoroff, tried his best to get the expulsion reversed, but to no avail.

Moshe went back to his orthodox roots in the Diaspora. When he found that he could not bear it any longer he returned to Palestine illegally by swimming from a ship as it neared the coast. Once he was back in his homeland he changed his surname from Blatt to Avineri and grew a moustache to disguise himself from the police.

Moshe's story won Mordechai's heart and the two became close friends. He was a frequent visitor to Chienke and Mordechai's home. Whenever Mirale noticed that there was watermelon in the house she would insist that a piece be left for "Avineri". Moshe met Rochke,

---

[31] A student in a religious seminary

102

Chienke's sister, at Chienke and Mordechai's home and a romance developed. Eventually, he joined Rochke's kibbutz, Ein Hashofet, where they lived and raised a family until he passed away in 1988.

Together, Moshe and Mordechai befriended Avadia, who was from Hungary. Avadia joined a traditional (religious) kibbutz of the Agudath Yisrael movement. When the kibbutz became defunct, most of the members went into business or became religious functionaries. However, Avadia remained true to the ideology of religion and work.

The three friends, Mordechai, Moshe and Avadia, and some of the other workers, were uneasy about the political and economic conditions of the late 1930s. The job they were working on would soon be finished, and the future looked bleak. Some of the former *kibbutzniks* thought of returning to that way of life. Others considered the possibility of organizing a cooperative, a moshav, similar to the one at Nahalal. They looked to Mordechai for advice because they knew that he was acquainted with leaders of the *moshav* movement.

So, early one Saturday morning, on his only day off when there was no public transportation, Mordechai left Chienke and Miriam to walk the thirty kilometers to Nahalal. He arrived late in the morning at the home of Tzvi Yehuda. There, he was welcomed with surprise at the distance he had walked. After refreshments and lunch, Mordechai explained to his host how he and a number of former *kibbutzniks*, who were working in the rock quarry near Haifa, were interested in starting a new moshav. Tzvi Yehuda listened with interest but when it came to practical matters he said that the Jewish Agency was short of the funds needed to support such a project. Each member would have to contribute five thousand dollars. Later, the amount needed dropped to one thousand dollars per member. Mordechai explained that even one hundred dollars was too much. At this Tzvi Yehuda suggested that they go to the community hall to discuss the matter with other members of the moshav, especially with Shmuel Dayan, the father of the future general, Moshe Dayan. The moshav members advised Mordechai to borrow one thousand dollars from his family in Montreal. This would make it possible to settle on an established moshav. The idea of starting a new settlement was too difficult in those times.

In the late afternoon, Mordechai started the long hike back to Hadar Hacarmel, where Chienke, Moshe and Avadia were waiting for his report. What they heard didn't make them very happy. For Mordechai and Chienke, the problem was acute. But which path should they take? Should they return to Gesher or perhaps join Degania, or should they join their original *Hashomer Hatzair* group, which was now living on a temporary kibbutz in Hadera? The thought of becoming ordinary city dwellers like many other workers did not occur to them. It was the idea of living a kibbutz life, or at least on a *moshav*, that motivated their *aliyah* to *Eretz Yisrael*. Although Mordechai and Chienke would have been gladly accepted by any kibbutz, it was difficult for them to go back to a situation they had left. In fact, they could have remained in Haifa.

In later visits, when Israel was already a state, they found that many of their friends had left the kibbutz (or *moshav*) and had established themselves in work or in business and lived in private homes. Because they did not take this possibility into account, Mordechai and Chienke made the wrong decision. Mordechai wrote to his father, David, to ask for a loan of one thousand dollars so that he and his family could settle on an established moshav. This decision had a considerable effect on their future lives, although, as will be shown, not on their ideological state of mind.

When Motl's father received the letter asking for a loan, he came to a different conclusion. He and his wife Freide were getting older and they very much wanted to see their youngest son Motl (in leaving the kibbutz Mordechai reverted to using his Diaspora name), whom they had not seen for six years, along with his capable wife Chienke, and their daughter Mirale, whom they had never seen. Instead of sending them a loan, he suggested sending them tickets for passage back to Montreal. These, he would have to purchase on a payment plan. Who had cash during the Depression? Both Motl and Chienke had thrown away their Canadian passports when they made *aliyah*, but fortunately they had kept their Canadian citizenship papers. They could come back for an extended visit and work to save up enough money to return and establish themselves in *Eretz Yisrael* again. Of course, Motl's father didn't foresee the outbreak of the Second World War in 1939.

Part 2: *Moving Back to Montreal*

At first, David suggested that Motl come back to Montreal by himself. He could work and save the money needed to bring Chienke and Miriam. But Motl refused to be separated from his family. Finally travel papers arrived for all three of them. This time it was hard to refuse. Motl's father had gone to a lot of trouble and expense and it was also likely that Motl's job in Haifa would be terminated. So at the last minute they made arrangements in the harbour to take a ship to Trieste, Italy. There, a travel agent of the Cunard line was to meet them to arrange their train travel to Paris. In Paris, Chienke and Motl and their Palestinian-born daughter had to get a special visa from the Canadian Consul.

It was a worrisome trip. Mirale was the only pleasure and encouragement they had. She was two years and ten months old, and a talented observer. When the ship neared Italy she noticed that the sky was cloudy. This was early November, 1937 and the skies in Palestine were still sunny. "Phooey," she said," why are the skies so dirty?" Soon she was noticed by all the passengers on the ship. Many of them were leaving the hardships of Palestine to return to Europe. Who knows what became of them during the Holocaust? Maybe Motl and Chienke were making a mistake too. But it was too late.

On the train to Paris Mirale continued to be the centre of attention, both to her parents and to the passengers. Chienke and Motl did their best to provide her with food and toys until they arrived at the Canadian Consul in Paris. Chienke and Motl were worried about the legality of their documents. However, just when the consul began to examine their papers and ask questions Mirale began to run around his office. She found a light switch and turned the lights off. When Motl and Chienke became angry at her, she said that she had to go to the bathroom. The consul sympathized with Mirale and played with her. In the confusion he gave them their visa without even looking at their papers.

They travelled from Paris to Le Havre by train and from there to Southampton, England on a small ship. There, they transferred to a larger ship for the trip to Montreal. On this last part of the trip they had time to relax. The sea was not stormy and Mirale could play. But Motl and Chienke were anxious at the thought of having left *Eretz Yisrael*, and they wondered how soon it would be before they returned.

When they arrived at the Port of Montreal, Chienke's two oldest sisters, Leah and Raizel, were waiting for them along with Odel, Motl's sister, and her husband Arke. Of course, they were taken straight away to see Motl's parents, David and Freide, for an emotional reunion. David and Freide were anxious to get to know Chienke, wife of their 'musinik', their youngest son, as well as their Hebrew-speaking granddaughter, Mirale. She became the centre of attention, making her cousin, who was about the same age, jealous and creating bad feelings between them right from the start.

The immediate problem was where the newcomers would stay until they could get settled. Motl's parents lived in a small apartment behind their grocery store on De Bullion Street. It was decided that Motl and his family would eat with them but they would have to sleep somewhere else. Sleeping arrangements were organized with Odel, and Arke, who lived on the same street. Odel and Arke were childless. They knew Motl's wife Chienke from their days in the Zionist youth movement and they adored their little niece. Odel and Arke lived in a flat with a double parlour. They found a crib for Mirale and she slept in their bedroom parlour. Motl and Chienke slept on a couch in the dining room parlour.

The first few weeks passed smoothly. Motl's parents were happy to see them at mealtimes. Once, when they were eating eggs, Mirale noticed that Chienke was served one too. In Haifa, eggs were scarce and only she and her hardworking father ate them. So Mirale said, in Hebrew, "Mother, even you are eating an egg!" Freide didn't understand Hebrew so they had to translate for her. In this way, Motl's parents learned about the hardships they experienced in Palestine. They began to feed them rich foods, so much so that Motl became ill. At the same time, Odel and Arke were so kind to Mirale that there was a possibility that she would become a spoiled child. They arranged a birthday party for her when she became three years old. She had already learned some English, so Arke taught her to make a little speech to the guests saying, "Today I am three years old. Whoever did not bring me a present can give me a cheque."

Chienke and Motl's friend Masha could see the potential problems. She advised them to find a place for themselves and to start to earn a living. Masha thought that they could rent a room from her mother and step-father. Her step-father was a carpenter who worked as a foreman for a firm that made wooden chesterfield (sofa) frames. He offered Motl a job that paid twelve dollars a week. That was not much, even for those times, but it was better than nothing. It was suggested that Chienke ask for work as a teacher for a Jewish orphanage in Westmount, a wealthier neighbourhood. That way she would be able to keep Mirale with her while she worked. But when Chienke visited the orphanage she did not like the atmosphere in the place and she would not have wanted to keep her child there. The only source of income she was left with was giving Hebrew lessons to a girl from a wealthy family that lived in Outremont.

Motl's job as a carpenter did not last long because the Jewish boss hinted that he wanted Motl to spy on his foreman. This Motl could not do, so he told his friend, Masha's step-father, and left the job. He found temporary work on a project that involved demolishing a sports arena located in the Mount Royal-St. Urbain Street area and reconstructing it as a factory. Here Motl received eighteen dollars a week.

Motl's parents were uneasy about their son's situation. Why should he and his family live in a room with older people and why rely on temporary jobs? As soon as a flat became available in their building they rented it to their children for seventeen dollars a month. Then Motl's father urged him to go into business for himself. He convinced Motl to buy a second-hand truck with money that he borrowed from the Hebrew Free Loan Society. Motl's brother Hershel and his brother-in-law Arke (Rochel's husband) were supposed to lend him the money for merchandise. Hershel refused outright, claiming that the 'chalutz' was too negligent. He would never be able to repay the money. With Arke's help, Motl did go into the wholesale fruit business. But it failed after a year. The second-hand truck gave more trouble than service.

Next, Hershel and Arke decided to get into the butcher business in addition to their fruit operation. They needed Motl's help so he was hired for eighteen dollars a week. But this too did not last long. The Second World War was breaking out and the partners were having trouble getting along.

It was the summer of 1939. The father of the young girl to whom Chienke was giving Hebrew lessons was giving her a ride home. When he asked about his daughter's progress Chienke suggested that he pay more attention to his daughter's studies. He explained that he was very busy as he had become the president of a congregation that was building a new synagogue, including a community centre and Hebrew school, in Outremont. When Motl heard about this new development he became interested. First, the idea of developing something new excited the *chalutz* in him. And then finding a steady job with enough income to save for the future was very important. He asked Chienke to recommend to the president that Motl be given the job as superintendent of the new synagogue complex. That the complex would include an apartment for the superintendent and his family was an added attraction to Motl. Chienke was surprised. She asked Motl if he thought he would like the job and whether his family would agree to it.

"Who are they to agree or disagree," asked Motl. "They did not agree when I went to work in Western Canada and they never understood why I wanted to become a *chalutz*. I am still the same *chalutz*, even in the Diaspora."

When Chienke asked the president of the new synagogue to help Motl get the job as superintendent, he too was surprised. He tried to suggest that Motl consider taking a job as a Hebrew teacher or as a *shamos* (sextant) rather than one usually given to a gentile. And what would his family say? Chienke explained that while Motl spoke fluent Hebrew, he had never been trained to teach, and while he had been raised in a traditional home, he was too secular-minded to become a shamos. She explained further that because of his experience on the kibbutz and his pioneering way of thinking Motl did not shy away from physical work. And besides, they needed a home and an income.

The president was impressed with Chienke's proposition and asked to meet Motl. When they did meet, Motl reminded him of his own youth in Moldavia when he too belonged to the *chalutz* movement. He decided to put Motl forward for the position, although most of the members of the synagogue were against the idea of hiring a Jew for that kind of work. They claimed that a Jew would be hard to manage because he may have his own ideas and be less obedient. This was Diaspora psychology at work. The newly appointed rabbi was hostile as well. He asked that Motl be asked to at least meet with the building committee, which he did. A few members of the committee, who were members of an organization that encouraged Hebrew culture, were pleased when they heard Motl speak fluent Hebrew, saying, "Why not have such a nice Jewish family live in our new synagogue building"? The chairman of the committee asked Motl to agree to consult with an engineer who worked for him on matters pertaining to the synagogue's boiler system. Since Motl felt that he might not be familiar with this system he agreed and was offered the position. Motl remembered that an old friend from the Poale Zion days now owned a soft drink company. He was introduced to the plant engineer who gave him lessons on how to run a large furnace. In this way, Motl felt more secure about his new job.

The new building was not ready yet. A ceremony for the laying of the cornerstone was held in the middle of the high holy days, just when the Second World War had started. Motl attended the sombre ceremony. The cantor said some prayers and the new rabbi, a handsome man in his forties, gave a sermon. He spoke about the war and about the cruelties experienced by the Jews of Eastern Europe. He ended with words to the effect that we will defend our country with one hand and we will build our synagogue with the other hand.

Now what about the rest of Motl and Chienke's families? What were their lives like in Montreal during the two years that preceded the war? Most of the members of Chienke's family were either unemployed or poor during the Depression. Raizel and her husband had to take care of Rivke and Isaac, and their daughter – another Miriam, who had returned to Montreal from Palestine three months before Motl and Chienke and *their* Miriam. Oishel (Harry) and his family were also not well off. Oishel could not understand why

Chienke had gone to Eretz Yisrael in the first place, and he wasn't very friendly. Itzel was unemployed. Leah was the one who showed a special interest in Chienke and Mirale. Although she had her own problems, she took Chienke and Mirale with her for summer vacation in the Laurentian Mountains while Motl stayed behind with his parents in the city to work. In general, during this period Motl and Chienke and their daughter Miriam were taken care of by Motl's parents and by Odel and Arke.

But what about all the *chaverim* that Motl and Chienke had left behind when they went to Palestine? The former members of the Chizhik Club, which had been led by Chienke before she left for Palestine, demonstrated special interest. During the intervening years they had grown up and matured. They understood Chienke and Motl's difficult situation, and they did more than the rest to provide friendship and support. Mirale, the quick observer, called them, in Yiddish, 'mothers girls'. Then there were Motl's friends, Itzik and Sylvia and Berl and Rivke, who were also helpful and friendly, even though they themselves led a poor life. Of the other friends, some were a little better off but many were poor themselves. They thought that Chienke and Motl's families would be able to take care of the "*yordim*', those who literally go down from *Eretz Yisrael*.

In fact, Motl and Chienke were going through a difficult period. Chienke became pregnant and because of neglect in medical treatment the child, a boy, was born sick and lived only one month. To arrange a burial cost money, at least fifty dollars, and Motl had none. He had to carry the child to the Baron de Hirsch Cemetery and dig the grave by himself. In spite of the difficulty, Motl was a *chalutz* and he managed to do it. But where were their friends and relatives? The only explanation is that the families were angry at Motl and Chienke for not having been more careful in their circumstances.

The Jewish situation during the immediate pre-war period was severe. Hitler's influence was felt in Quebec. In response to the threats made by fascists like Adrian Arcand, a popular pre-war French Canadian nationalist and anti-semite, and his followers, the Canadian Jewish Congress organized resistance groups made up of young Jewish men. The Poale Zion movement played a major role in this matter. Motl's close friends tried to pull him back into the social life of the Diaspora, but after spending several years in *Eretz Yisrael* it was some time before he could get involved again.

The Farband became the social arm of the Poale Zion movement. Motl's close friend Itzik became deeply involved in the Farband after being disappointed with the Left Poale Zion. He tried to convince Motl to join, but to Motl it was only a society for cemetery rights and fundraising purposes. To him it seemed to lack friendliness and he could not afford the cost of belonging anyway. But Itzik warned, "Wait, when you are more settled, we'll get you."

Chienke, on the other hand, joined the Migdal group of the Pioneer Women Organization as soon as Motl's sister Rochel suggested it. Perhaps women are more ideologically flexible. In any case, a social life was costly so Motl and Chienke spent most of their time with Motl's parents and with Odel and Arke, their nearest neighbours. Father was writing his memoirs, and from time to time he would read what he had written. They often went on walks with Mother and Mirale on Fletcher's Field near Mount Royal. When they passed the Jewish home for the aged, Mirale would ask, "*Ma Zeh?*" (Hebrew for "what is this?"). Chienke told her that it was a home where children put their parents when they became old, as she would when they, Motl and Chienke, became old. Miriam, who was only four years old, said, "No, I will not. I will need you to take care of my children."

Part 3: The Synagogue Years

This is the situation that Motl and Chienke were in until they moved into an apartment in the basement of the newly built Adath Israel Synagogue. The apartment was a modern one with two bedrooms, one for Miriam and one for Chienke and Motl. It had a living room and a modern kitchen with a refrigerator and a gas stove.

The Adath Israel Congregation included, at first, an afternoon Hebrew school that was later extended to a day school. Still later, a

Hebrew high school, the Adath Israel Academy, was added. Motl and Chienke and their children, Miriam at first and later a son, Jacob, were a part of the Adath Israel scene from January, 1940 until June, 1952.

Jacob's Commentary

As a child, and later in my life, I heard many of the episodes referred to in this chapter on numerous occasions. It has always been clear to me that this transition period of their lives was a difficult pill for my parents to swallow. They were giving up their dream of a pioneering life to return to safer but much less fulfilling lives back in the Diaspora they were from. Although they told themselves that it was temporary and that they were following their families' wishes, I think they both knew that it would a long time before they returned to Palestine. In fact, the first return visit they made to Israel was in 1966, 29 years after they left.

The Canada they came back to was far different than the one they left. The friends and relatives they had left behind were no longer as youthful and hopeful as they had been in earlier days. The lingering effects of the Great Depression were still being felt and now the country was approaching another major international conflict, World War II. Motl had no recognized trade to help him find a job. He was fortunate that, after struggling and moving from one temporary job to another for almost two years, he was able, with my mother's help, to get the job as superintendent of a synagogue/Hebrew school complex.

The part of the story dealing with the tragic birth and death of a little boy after their return to Montreal was a very painful and bitter experience. I didn't know about this at all until my mother let something slip when I was in my late teens and she and I were driving around doing the collection for my father's business. We were doing it because he was sick and I was old enough to drive. At some point my mother said. "It's too bad that Avrum isn't here." The baby had been named after my father's brother, who was killed in the pogrom that took place in their *shtetl* after World War I. Neither my parents nor my sister would talk about this episode. However, I did learn that the child was born with a heart defect and that he lived, as the chapter notes, for about a month. This fact, that he only lived for about a month, may have been a factor, since a child is expected to be at least a month in age for a Jewish burial and shiva (mourning) to take place. When my father did mention this event in his later years and after my mother died, it was clear that he still felt bitter about it. It certainly helps me to understand why my parents were so protective and concerned about my health, especially during my early childhood.

As I already noted at the end of the last chapter, my parents didn't get back to visit Palestine until 1966, well after the establishment of the State of Israel. They went to Israel several times after that, until age made long distance travel impossible. After all, my mother's youngest sister Rochke was there and the two sisters missed each other terribly. One of their longer visits coincided with the 10-month sabbatical period I referred to earlier in 1978-79, when I and my wife and children first visited Israel. We visited Israel several times after that, including two summer-long visits that took place in 1982 and 1983. Our ten-month initial visit gave us ample time to see many of the sites that are noted in my parents' memoirs of their stay in *Eretz Yisrael*. I recall the pleasure I had when we discovered that the quarry my father worked at after leaving kibbutz life, still existed! Indeed, it is located near the top of Mount Carmel, just north of the main road joining Haifa and the Jezreel Valley.

This is the same road we took when we drove from our rented apartment on the Carmel to visit my aunt, uncle and cousins in Kibbutz Ein Hashofet. Ein Hashofet, named after US Supreme Court Justice Brandeis, was created in 1937 at about the time when my parents and sister were leaving Palestine. My aunt, Rochke, and her husband, Moishe Avineri, who my father described in this chapter, were among the original group of pioneers, and they remained there for the rest of their lives. My family and I visited often and it gave us a taste of the communal lifestyle that a kibbutz exemplified. Meals were taken in a communal dining hall and children were still housed away from their parents in a home for children. Most of our visits were made on Saturdays and we would often see young children being wheeled in moveable playpens from the children's home to their parents' cottage. At that time the kibbutz raised avocados and included two factories, one that made screws and another that fashioned the ballasts needed for fluorescent light bulbs. There was a full sized swimming pool and a concert hall as well. My aunt taught Hebrew for many years in an *Ulpan* (a program designed to teach Hebrew to new immigrants) that was run by the kibbutz. The program of study lasts five months and students live and work on the kibbutz. Because my aunt spoke English fluently, she was a very popular teacher among North American immigrants.

My parents visited Israel for about two months during our ten-month stay. During that time, we made a number of day trips with them to places that recalled their years in the 1930s. We visited Kibbutz Ramat Yohanan, where my father stayed and worked for a while after he first arrived in Eretz Yisrael. We also visited Kibbutz Degania, my mother's first kibbutz, and my father's cousin Ada in Safed, whom he visited in his first year in Eretz Yisrael when she lived in Kfar Giladi. The one place my parents and I didn't go to was Kibbutz Ashdod Yaakov, the kibbutz my parents left in the late 1930s.

This chapter refers to Arlosoroff, the political head of the Jewish Agency, and this brings up an important and sensational historical episode. Chaim Arlosoroff was born in Ukraine and educated as an economist in Germany. He immigrated to Palestine in 1924 and quickly rose in the ranks of the Mapai party, the dominant labour-oriented political group among Palestinian Jews. Mapai dominated politics in Israel until Begin was elected in 1977. As political head of the Jewish Agency, a pre-state quasi-governmental organization, he was responsible for negotiating the Transfer Agreement with the German government, as related in chapter 4. He was assassinated on the beach in Tel Aviv in 1933, just two days after returning from Germany. The nationalistic right wing Zionist Revisionists were blamed for the murder and three of its members were arrested. All were acquitted and the murder has remained an enigma, one that has resulted in a number of conspiracy theories but no solution. The Begin Government formally investigated the murder in 1982, well after it took place. The inquiry concluded that the men arrested had nothing to do with it, but it offered no new insights as to who was responsible.

Chapter 6: The Adath Israel Congregation

Part 1: *Before and During the War*

This chapter describes the thirteen years experienced by Motl and his family in association with the Adath Israel complex, which included a synagogue, a community centre, a Hebrew afternoon and day school and, finally, a Hebrew high school academy. The development of the Adath Israel was a part of the two hundred year history of the development of Jewish life in Canada, particularly in the city of Montreal. It began with the arrival of the first Sephardic settlers and the construction of the first Spanish and Portuguese Synagogue on Notre Dame Street East, within sight of the Quebec Courthouse. They were followed by German Jewish immigrants and the Shaar Hashomayim Synagogue. Later, a Hungarian *shul* was established on Notre Dame West, near the Lachine Canal, a Galitzianer on Milton, a Romanian on Duluth, a Russian on Fairmount, and so on.

The Adath Israel was the first congregation in Montreal to be established without nostalgic connections overseas. In the late nineteen thirties a new Jewish class of professionals, manufacturers and businessmen had appeared. They were for the most part Canadian-born or, in a few cases, new arrivals from England. They shared the desire to leave the Jewish ghetto of east-central Montreal in order to live in the posh and more landscaped surroundings of Outremont, a suburb on the north slope of Mount Royal.

This move created the traditional Jewish need of establishing a prayerhouse for daily as well as Sabbath and holiday services, and a school (*cheder*) to prepare children for their *bar* and *bat mitzvahs*. At first, a flat was rented above a row of stores on Van Horne Street. There was no rabbi, only a combination cantor and teacher, who conducted services and taught Hebrew to the children. Later, when the community expanded, a decision to build a modern sanctuary, which would include a community centre and a Hebrew afternoon school, was made.

By the end of 1939 the new sanctuary was near completion. The eastern section containing offices, a daily chapel and, most importantly, the superintendent's apartment, was finished first so that Motl and his family could move in to help supervise the transfer of the building from the contracters.

Motl, with Chienke and Miriam, moved in January, 1940. The new building was located on a lot measuring approximately 100 by 300 feet on the northern side of Outremont. It was bounded by McEachran Street on the west, Ducharme on the north, Dollard on the east and a lane along the south side.

The main entrance to the sanctuary was on McEachran. It was landscaped with grass, trees and bushes and consisted of six concrete steps and square columns leading to a red tiled patio about fifteen feet deep. The roof, twenty feet above the entrance, included Hebrew and English inscriptions, with a Star of David in the middle. Stained glass windows with biblical designs adorned each side of the entrance, as well as the length of the sanctuary. The entrance itself consisted of three double doors of dark oak, the same wood that framed the stained glass windows and formed the benches inside the sanctuary. The floor and walls of the lobby, about fifteen feet in depth and twenty feet in height, were covered with sand-coloured marble.

The eastern side of the lobby included the two main doors, which opened into the sanctuary. Two copper tablets, located between the doors, were inscribed with the names of contributors and synagogue activists. In keeping with the spirit of Canadian democracy, the names were listed alphabetically and not according to position or size of contribution. Doors on either side of the main ones and a few steps up led to the women's sections of the sanctuary. The southern side of the lobby included the lady's washroom and stairs to the sanctuary balcony located above the lobby. Another set of stairs from the opposite side of the lobby also led to the balcony. A special office and reception room, used for the signing of marriage contracts, was located part of the way up these stairs. The wedding parties, led by the rabbi and cantors, marched from these rooms to the central *Bima* of the sanctuary.

The sanctuary itself was about 24 feet in height and 80 feet wide. The central portion, measuring 50 by 60 feet, contained three rows of benches on a side for male members of the congregation. The *Bima* was a raised platform, 10 feet by 10 feet, situated in the middle of this central area. The cantor prayed and read the Torah from a desk on the *Bima*. The rabbi and cantor sat on the right and left sides of a bench placed opposite the desk, while those receiving *aliyahs* (honours) sat between them. The space between the *Bima* and the Ark on the eastern wall of the sanctuary was an open area with three rows of benches, each with 12 seats, on either side. The most active members sat in these seats. In all, the sanctuary contained 450 seats for male members. The women sat in two raised areas located along the stained glass windows on either side of the sanctuary. A four-inch chromium pipe topped the *mechitza* that separated the women's sections from the area where the men sat. Wives of the more active members of the congregation sat opposite the Ark on the northern and southern sides of the sanctuary.

Three marble steps led to a six-foot wide marble platform in front of the Ark on the eastern wall of the sanctuary. Chairs for the president and *parness*, a lay religious leader of the synagogue, and the two vice-presidents were placed on either side of the ark, while a dais that the rabbi would use during his sermons was on the right side. The Ark itself, three feet deep, was lit with flourescent lights and covered with a white tapestry. A wooden grill above the Ark hid a choir room located on an upper level, east of the sanctuary.

A door from the eastern wall of the sanctuary also led to a twenty-by-twenty-foot chapel, used for daily services, as well as synagogue offices, a boardroom, and an outer door to Ducharme Street. The second floor of this part of the building included four classrooms for the afternoon Hebrew school and the choir room overlooking the sanctuary.

A semi-basement extended for the full length of the building from west to east. Stairs from the sanctuary lobby led down to another lobby leading to a large assembly hall, located below the sanctuary. This lobby included men's and ladies' washrooms on either end, and a central checking room. The assembly hall extended below the full length and width of the sanctuary, although the height from floor to ceiling was only twelve feet. Windows along the north and south walls faced Ducharme Street and the lane behind the building. The centre of the east side of the hall contained a stage, which led to a passage and a door to Ducharme Street. To the right of the stage, a door led to the main kitchen while another one on the left opened to a dairy kitchen and service room. This part of the building also contained a furnace room and a room where the superintendent could store tools and stock.

The superintendent's apartment was located below the synagogue offices, two steps up from the main hall. It consisted of a master bedroom looking out onto Ducharme, a kitchen and bathroom, another bedroom and a living room overlooking a large garden and landscaped area, which contained a temporary *Sukkah*. Here, until 1946, after the end of the Second World War, Motl and Chienke and Miriam (and from 1944 on, Yankale) spent their days and nights.

The other workers in the building included, of course, the rabbi, who was at first more like an executive director, since the sanctuary was not finished, and the cantor, who moved from the flat on Van Horne Street to establish daily services in the chapel. Services were attended mainly by elderly Jews living in the neighborhood and by younger mourners saying *Kaddish*, the mourning prayer.

Motl's main job concerned the maintenance of the building. He was not supposed to have much to do with the clergy. However, as soon as he moved in he became involved with a problem in the chapel. The cantor, who was also a reverend capable of providing religious services, was subservient to the rabbi's religious authority in the new building. In sanctuary services, the cantor was now left with providing the cantorial singing (the job of *chazan sheini*; literally, "second cantor"), reading the Torah and being the *shammas* (sextant). The cantor's sphere of influence now centred on the chapel, where he was responsible for daily services, mainly with the elderly who were called for minyans and Talmud study and for Saturday afternoon and evening services, including the third Sabbath meal, *shalosh se'udot*. The cantor was supposed to open the chapel early in the morning in time for the first service. He was also supposed to be available during the day, to deal with spiritual questions and to be on hand until after evening services. The problem was that the cantor didn't arrive early enough to open the door to the chapel for the early arrivals, so the elderly congregants began to knock on Motl's window. At first it was five o'clock in the morning, then four-thirty and then four, as they competed for the honour of being the first to prayers. This could not go on. Motl and his family couldn't get a full night's sleep. Motl's solution was to make keys for the devoted elderly so that they could let themselves into the chapel.

Motl couldn't remove himself entirely from religious matters. After all, he was Jewish and he spoke Yiddish and Hebrew, as did Chienke and Miriam. When a male was needed for a *minyan*, they called Motl and when it was after hours and someone needed information concerning matters of a traditional nature, Chienke was always at hand. There came a point when the president was visiting Chienke and Motl, one evening, and Chienke answered a telephone call. The caller said that he had received a reminder to say *Kaddish* on a certain day, but he was sure that the proper date was the next day. Chienke asked why the caller could not say *Kaddish* on both days! The president was amazed at the complexity of the situation.

Motl was tolerant, and didn't let himself get too entangled in the cantor's business. They remained friends throughout their years of working together. However, the situation between the rabbi and the cantor was another matter. The cantor came from a traditional orthodox background and while the rabbi was also orthodox, he was modern and hated the cantor's folksy old-country style. The antagonism went on for years until the cantor was forced to resign, an embittered and sick man.

The third colleague of Motl's was a young woman who worked in the office and came from the same orthodox family as the cantor. She was Chienke and Motl's age, and the three of them became close friends. Her job was to arrange contracts for various social and religious functions and then turn the implimentation of the contracts over to Motl. Motl organized rehearsals for weddings and bar mitzvahs; he made sketches of the table arrangements, handled all of the purchasing of food and drink and other items and never asked to be tipped for his services. In return, Motl received the clothes checking concession, with a right to charge fifteen cents per person. If Motl needed materials for maintenance work, the woman in the office ordered it for him. When Motl received the goods he signed the receipts, giving one copy to the office and keeping one for himself. This arrangement worked smoothly for years until the woman who handled office matters became ill and had to leave her job.

When Motl accepted the job as superintendent he had promised the chairman of the building committee that he would ask for help from his (the chairman's) engineer in running the big coal furnace and boiler. Motl decided not to rely on the chairman's engineer. He had a friend from his *Poale Zion* days who was now the owner of a soft drink company. Motl befriended the plant engineer, who came to the synagogue and explained the operation of the furnace to Motl. The chairman's engineer was left with little to do.

One day, Motl received delivery of galvanized garbage cans ordered by the chairman's engineer. The order was for twelve cans but only six were delivered. Motl refused to sign the receipt and sent the six cans back. The next day the chairman and the president asked Motl why he didn't cooperate with the engineer as he had promised when he took the job. Motl was outraged and he answered, "When I drive the car, I alone have to hold the steering wheel." Motl took a big risk, for if the president was not tuned in to what was actually going on, the chairman would have fired him outright—and then where would Motl and Chienke go, and how would they make a living? Fortunately, the president got the point. The next day he came to Motl and told him to do the job as he saw fit.

During the winter of 1940, Motl's job was to attend to the furnace and to take over from the contractors as the finishing touches were made to the entire building. Only after Purim did Sabbath services commence in the sanctuary. In previous years, Motl and Chienke celebrated Passover with Motl's parents. Now that they were living further away they decided to celebrate by themselves. Mirale was already five years old, old enough for Chienke to teach her the Four Questions and how to set the Passover table. When the president came after evening services to wish them a good holiday and saw the set table, he returned to the rabbi and the others and told them to go and see for themselves how to prepare for the Seder. When they saw it for themselves, one of the members said, "Are we not fortunate to have such a Jewish family living in our *shul*?"

From Passover until Lag B'Omer, synagogue celebrations were curtailed. However, during this period the principal of the Hebrew afternoon school arrived. He was actually not a stranger since he came from a town in Lithuania, close to the one that Chienke was from, and Motl knew him as a *Poale Zion* sympathizer and a Hebrew and Yiddish intellectual. Chienke and Motl conversed with him in Hebrew and Yiddish, and he adored Mirale. So did the rabbi, although he was a more reserved and arrogant man. Motl was needed to help in the preparation for the school's opening in September 1940. His experience in building a school during his kibbutz years turned out to be very useful. However, there was some conflict because the principal could be negligent, particularly when it came to planning, and Motl had too many other responsibilities to afford to waste time. Nevertheless, working on the school was the most satisfying part of Motl's job.

The first wedding celebration in the new synagogue was held on Lag Baomer, and then after Shavuoth the weddings and bar and bat mitzvahs began in earnest. The Adath Israel became an important institution in the social life of Montreal Jews. With the exception of the Shaar Hashamayim Synagogue and Temple Emanuel, there were no other modern synagogue structures. The personality of the rabbi and the material prosperity of wartime Canada added to the prominence of the Adath Israel Congregation.

Up to this point, Motl did not need to hire any additional help. He managed to do the work by himself. But with the increase in the number of catered affairs he needed help with cleaning and dishwashing after each celebration so as to be ready for the next one. Motl made an arrangement with a woman of Slovakian origin, Annie, who worked for one of the caterers, to remain behind after serving the meals to wash the dishes. An Irish gardener named Mike who lived in the neighborhood helped out in with extra general work.

In time, Motl needed still more help. Mike introduced him to two milkmen who were willing to work after their regular jobs, from early in the afternoon until late in the evening, even later than midnight. They were happy with their pay of one dollar an hour plus any liquor that the bartenders left behind, provided of course that that there was no drinking on the job. This trio remained Motl's friends even after he left the synagogue and went into business for himself.

The continuing increase in the number of functions at the synagogue meant that Annie could not handle the dishwashing on her own. She recommended that Motl hire another Slovak woman, also named Annie, Annie B. Annie B. arrived in Montreal with a husband, two daughters and a son just before the Second World War. Her husband was a hard working, hard drinking man who worked as a cooper[32] for a company in Montreal's east end. Annie B. was always in need of extra earnings. She became a good friend to Motl and Chienke and a babysitter, first for Mirale and later for Yankale.

One morning a blond, good-looking young woman came to visit Motl. She introduced herself as Mary, Annie B.'s daughter. Mary explained that her father was always accusing his wife of being too friendly to Motl so she decided to see for herself. Motl invited her into his apartment, introduced her Chienke and Mirale, and asked if she thought her father should be taken seriously. She responded by asking if she and her husband, George, could also work for Motl in their spare time. Mary and George and Motl and Chienke were friends for many years.

Until Mary's visit, Motl's job in the checking room required help from Chienke. But Motl did not want Chienke to get too involved, as he preferred that she look after Mirale and later, Yankale. So Chienke's brother Itzel, who was often out of work, or Chienke's sister Reizel's sons, two schoolboys named Gershon and Morris, would work at the checking. Sometimes a neighbor boy, Bernard, would help. The trouble was that help of this kind meant reduced income for Motl. So Motl arranged for Mary to work at the checking

---

[32] A barrel maker

for the same rate of pay, one dollar per hour, paid for regular synagogue work. This arrangement continued for the rest of Motl's association with the Adath Israel Congregation. Not just Mary, but also George, Annie B., another Mary, and other relatives, all Slovaks, became checking-room assistants. They all remained Chienke and Motl's friends even after Motl left the synagogue. When Motl became an installment merchant they became supporters and customers.

There is another story involving the dishwashing/checking-room assistants. In return for Chienke's unpaid work, such as providing a 24-hour a day answering service, Motl felt it was fair to ask the synagogue workers for occasional cleaning or babysitting help for Chienke. One time, the president of the synagogue sisterhood, who was fond of Chienke and Motl and grateful for Motl's work for sisterhood functions, gave the two of them tickets to the opera. None of the Slovak women could babysit, as they had a wedding to attend. Motl arranged for a temporary worker, a French Canadian woman, to stay with the children. On their way in the taxi Chienke asked Motl how well he knew the woman. When Motl replied that he didn't know her at all, they turned back home. Some days later the sisterhood president asked how he had enjoyed the opera. When Motl told her what had happened she said, "Never mind, your own story is more meaningful than the opera."

The summer went by and preparations for the high holidays began. First there was the sale of reserved seats in the new sanctuary for the regular membership. For several weeks before Rosh Hashana members could register for seats in the sanctuary lobby on Sundays and evenings. Now an interesting example of hypocrisy developed. Before the synagogue was built, neighboring Jews and non-Jews had petitioned the City of Outremont to prevent its construction because they felt that property values would fall. Now the same Jews were asking for seats for the High Holidays. After some discussion, it was decided that Jews were Jews, even if they had sinned, and they were entitled to purchase seats, but only in the temporary sanctuary downstairs.

The organizing and setting up the temporary sanctuary was part of Motl's job. Although the ceiling was lower (12 feet instead of

24) the dimensions were the same as those of the permanent sanctuary. Every effort was made to ensure that those who prayed in the temporary sanctuary would not feel that they were second-class. The Ark from the days when the synagogue was on Van Horne was set up on the stage. With the help of charts that he drew on cardboard and plywood, Motl organized the seating arrangements so as to be a duplicate of the main sanctuary. The committee that sold the seats was given an enumerated plan of the seats. A few days before the holidays, Motl and his assistants erected a temporary *Bima*. Benches from the previous synagogue were placed around it. To keep the chairs from moving and shifting during the services, they were fixed in place with iron bars.

The seats in the main sanctuary were only sold during the first year. From then on the seatholders simply repeated their registration yearly through the synagogue office. However, seats for the temporary sanctuary downstairs were sold in the same manner every year, beginning a few weeks before the holidays. Motl, whose presence was required during these evenings, found it interesting to observe the goings on. Many purchasers asked why the price was so high. The committee members responded by saying, "Who says you have to only attend services for three days? The sanctuary and the chapel will welcome you year round."

Motl also noticed that some of the neighbors from the surrounding streets liked to come in to socialize and discuss current events. One of these was Motl's friend Moishe, who came in to buy seats for himself and his family on the first evening of the sales. Chienke and Motl had reserved seats in the temporary sanctuary, but Chienke was often busy taking care of Mirale (and later Yankale) and Motl found that it was best if he was not too visible if he wanted to avoid being continually pestered. He used to stroll around the synagogue. One day, he tried to find his friend Moishe but could not see him anywhere in *shul*. He rang his friend's doorbell but there was no answer. After the holidays Motl asked him what had happened. Moishe told Motl how he missed buying seats one year and went fishing instead. But by the time of Yom Kippur his consience troubled him badly. So now he never misses buying seats for the high holidays but he still goes fishing, his favorite recreation! This was only one of the unusual situations that Motl and Chienke experienced while living among the walls of Adath Israel.

Approximately 1500 people attended High Holiday services at Adath Israel during the war years. Right after Yom Kippur, Motl and his assistants dismantled the temporary sanctuary and began to assemble the prefabricated *Sukkah* on the lawn beside the windows of Chienke and Motl's apartment. The decorating was supposed to be the responsibility of the sisterhood, the teachers and the older children; but without Motl's help it wouldn't have happened.

The end of the High Holiday activities came with *Hoshana Rabba* and *Shmini Atzereth*, when *Yizkor* is said; but the main excitement was on *Simchat Torah*. The tradionalist and cultured members of the synagogue expected the teachers to lead the schoolchildren in parade, singing and waving flags and following the Torahs, but the teachers never showed up! Educational matters were left to the rabbi and principal while the officers of the synagogue only got involved in education in the financial sense. As a result, the teachers only considered themselves to be salaried employees of the school, and rarely showed up for Saturday or *Yom Tov* services.

Without the teachers' presence the children became very noisy and out of control. The rabbi couldn't take it. He became angry, dropped the *siddur*[33] and left the synagogue. Fortunately, the president did not lose himself. He came to the Bima and said, "We still have a *minyan*[34] let's continue the service."

The afternoon Hebrew school started right after *Shabbos Bereshet*, the Sabbath after the beginning of Genesis in the new year's reading of the Torah. The school had to use the large hall beneath the

---

[33] Prayerbook.

[34] Quorum.

sanctuary for assemblies until the end of the war. In the mornings there was a kindergarten, while on the weekends boys and girls were taught their bar and bat mitzvahs. With Saturday *kiddushim* and various celebrations on Saturday afternoon and evenings and then weddings on Sunday, the Adath Israel was a busy place. The war brought prosperity and many flaunted their newfound wealth in these affairs despite the seriousness of the war.

When the war started Motl was exempted from conscription because he was married and had a child. Many of Motl's friends were conscripted and some volunteered for the army. The Rabbi of the congregation served as a chaplain for the Jewish servicemen. He had the sorrowful duty of informing families of the wounding or death of their loved ones. At the beginning the casualties were light, but there were enough to break the heart of even strong characters such as the rabbi. In his sermons he tried to enlighten the congregation as to the seriousness of the situation in Europe. But few listened and the parties and family functions continued. Finally, at the congregation's Purim feast the Rabbi told the following story: It was the day of mourning for the destruction of the temple, *Tisha B'Av*. After a day of fasting some very pious Jews remained in *shul* to pray all night. After a while, it became boring so someone suggested that they have a drop to drink. One drop led to another and after a while they began to dance and sing, "It is the destruction of the temple so let's be happy!" The audience got the Rabbi's message. Some felt insulted. Those in the audience thought, "This Rabbi could be a hard man."

In time, the war situation became worse, even for Canada, and it was announced that after a certain date even married men could be conscripted. This led to a rush of weddings. The cantor had been qualified to perform weddings from the time of the previous synagogue and he continued to perform them on his own. The Rabbi wanted some help with his weddings so he asked Motl to assist as a witness. Motl did it out of interest. He wasn't reimbursed for his help. The Rabbi told him about one caller, a man, who asked if the Rabbi would marry him if his partner was a *shikse* (a gentile woman) because he had no Jewish girlfriends. The Rabbi responded. "How can you have a Jewish girlfriend if you run around with *shikses*?"

One positive effect of the war on Adath Israel Congregation was the arrival of the first Jewish refugees from Shanghai and Japan, in 1941-42. The first to come were two groups of young men from *yeshivas*. One group of Lubavitch *chasidim* under the leadership of Rabbi Mordechai was welcomed to Adath Israel; but they could not adjust to the style of a modern orthodox rabbi. With the help and encouragement of the more traditional members of the congregation, including the president, they created a Lubavich yeshiva in Montreal.

The second group was made up of *misnagdim* (not chasidic), and was led by Rabbi Menachem. Rabbi Menachem's story was tragic. When the Germans invaded, he escaped, leaving behind his wife and children. When Motl asked how he could leave them, he answered, "Who could have predicted that the the Germans would resort to annihilating women and children?" Although he was a traditional orthodox rabbi with a beard, Rabbi Menachem was the same age as Chienke and Motl and a close friendship developed between them.

With the help of supporters among the congregation, Rabbi Menachem also founded a yeshiva in Montreal: Yeshiva Merkaz Torah. However, a short time later he was invited to become the head (Rosh Yeshiva) of Yeshiva University in New York. Many years later when Chienke and Motl were vacationing in Saratoga Springs they met Rabbi Menachem again. He had remarried and had more children, but he looked old and his beard was grey and the tragedy of his past was still evident.

The war ended in 1945 but with the joy of the victory came the terrible news of the murder of six million Jews, including Chienke's eldest brother Hirshel, his wife and their three children.

Part 2: After the War

The superintendent's apartment was on the eastern end of the building, near the garden that extended to Dollard Street. It was decided that an extension to house a full- time Hebrew school and the kindergarten would be built on this site. It would contain a second lower level hall with four upper stories that would include sixteen classrooms, as well as a library, offices and a permanent suka. A larger and more modern apartment for the superintendent and the lobby to the new hall would contain windows and a door facing Ducharme Street.

It was estimated that it would take eighteen months to build the extension. The question was where would the superintendent and his family live in the meantime? Housing in Montreal was in very short supply after the war. There were no apartments available in the neighborhood of the synagogue. Fortunately, the president owned a modern apartment in the suburb of Hampstead. He agreed to rent it to the congregation for temporary use by Motl and his family.

Hampstead is a suburb located six miles west of the site of the synagogue. Although the move was a temporary one, it was in many ways a wonderful change for Chienke and the two children, Mirale and Yankale. They lived in a modern private apartment in one of the wealthier parts of Montreal; but for Motl the situation was made harder. The number of events in the synagogue multiplied. In addition to family affairs, such as bar mitzvahs and weddings and Hebrew school assemblies, the Adath Israel became the primary centre for a large number of organizations, including the congregation's sisterhood and brotherhood, the Zionist Federation, Hadassah, Keren Hatarbut (an adult learning centre for modern Hebrew), Bnai Brith, Knights of Pythias (a non-sectarian and international fraternal organization), *Vaad Hachinuch* (Jewish Educational Committee), and so on. The one available hall was busy day and night and as a result Motl hardly had time to see Chienke or the children. He and Chienke began to wonder if it was time to look for another job.

The new apartment in Hampstead also created problems for Mirale. She was ten years old and should have gone to the local school. However, the school had an exclusion policy and only White Anglo-Saxon Protestants could attend. Mirale had no choice but to be registered in a public school in Notre Dame de Grace, a nearby district of Montreal. This meant that she had a long walk through empty fields to get to and from school. After snowfalls, she had to make her way through deep drifts of uncleared snow. Motl couldn't help. He left for work very early in the morning, and Chienke had to look after Yankale. On weekends the neighborhood children teased Mirale for going to a different school. She answered that she went to another school because, "My parents say that you are bad children."

Now we will go back in time to describe what happened to the rest of Chienke and Motl's families during the period from 1940 until 1947, when Chienke and Motl and their children moved back into the synagogue. At first, when Chienke and Motl moved into the synagogue they were more or less ignored by their families. The reason for this may have had something to do with a mixture of snobishness and pity: "Look how the *chalutzim* have ended up!" Of course, Motl's parents did not lose interest in their youngest son and his family. At this time (1940) Motl developed pyorrhea, a disease of the gums. Right after Passover, he had to have all his teeth extracted and his gums painfully scraped so that he could be fitted with dentures. His parents ran back and forth to help, as did Chienke's sister Rivke who came to help when Motl had to visit the doctors. Chienke's "girls" from the Chizhik group were, as always, very nice.

In time, there were rumors that Motl and Chienke were becoming rich, but these were only rumors. However, Motl's sister Odel and her husband Arke did become wealthy during the war. They adopted a child, Fruma, and they could afford to buy luxury goods and take vacations during the summer and winter. When Yankale was born, they didn't even show up at his *bris*.[35] On the other hand, Chienke's brother Itzel was always in need and Chienke and Motl tried to help him as generously as they could.

Motl's brother Hershel found that the war did not bring prosperity to his fruit business. He needed to buy very large quantities to make a profit. When he asked Motl and Chienke to lend him $500 so that he could buy a carload of apples they were happy to make the loan, without interest. Hershel and his wife Chaike became close to

---

[35] Circumcision.

129

Motl and Chienke. When Yankale was born in 1944, they took Mirale with them to their summer home in the country. However, their own children were jealous of the special attention the visitor was getting and Mirale had to be taken home before the end of the summer. On another occasion, they took Motl and Mirale with them on a drive to visit Bela (Motl's eldest sister, Sorke's daughter) and her husband in Gloversville, New York.

There were a number of life-cycle events in the families during this period, including births, bar mitzvahs, and weddings. Last, but not least, there was the birth of Yaakov Gershon (Yankale), a son for Chienke and Motl and a brother for Mirale.

Because of wartime complications Yankale's *bris* had to be held in the synagogue rather than the hospital. It was a big event for the synagogue: the bris of a son of the only full-time residents of their *shul*! A number of the chapel faithful and officers of the synagogue were present, as were most of Motl and Chienke's families and close friends. When Motl found that he didn't have enough liquor for such a large group he approached one of the synagogue officials to see if he had a few bottles to lend him. The official was surprised: "You, of all people should have plenty of bottles from the various affairs and from dealing with the bartenders." He meant that it was commonly understood that synagogue caretakers stole on the job and it was naive of Motl not to do the same. In fact, he admired Motl's honesty and he brought several of his own bottles while refusing to accept payment.

During the *bris*, Chienke's sisters Leah and Rivke were bustling about to see to it that the baby was properly named, after their father and grandfather. Meanwhile, Chienke kept reminding Motl to say the blessing that the father is supposed to say. In all the fuss and excitment Motl forgot to say it. Although he was not very observant, he told the mohel that he forgot the blessing and asked him what he should do. The *mohel* said, "Say it now!"

While living temporarily in Hampstead, Motl and Chienke began to think seriously of making a change to a life that would give them more privacy. Perhaps they should move back to *Eretz Yisrael* and a life on a *moshav*. Now they had some savings of their own and they knew what to expect in Palestine. Mirale was eleven years and could still speak Hebrew while Yankale was too young (only two) to be affected. Motl's parents thought it was a fine idea, but only on condition that they come along too. They could not bear to be separated from Motl and Chienke and their children. Even when Chienke tried to describe the hardships and privations of life in Palestine they would not change their minds. By this time they were in their mid-seventies. Father had a heart condition and Mother had had a stroke that affected one-half of her face, and so another of Motl's and Chienke's dreams faded.

Motl tried another idea. From his job in the synagogue, he became familiar with the supplies needed for affairs. While still living in the Adath Israel he decided to try to set up a rental business that would provide tables, benches, dishes and cutlery for halls and synagogues that were in short supply of such goods. He bought some stock from a warehouse for $1000 and stored it in a shed behind his father's store. Motl would get the orders and Itzel was supposed to make the deliveries. But it didn't work. Itzel was not suited for that type of work and Motl was left with the stock.

Another business possibility involved Odel's husband Arke who had become quite prosperous dealing in jewelery during the war. Arke could have used Motl's organizational ability (and the investment he could make) in order to cope with the increased business competition of the postwar years, but Arke could not understand that times had changed and nothing came of this.

At this time, Motl's sister Chaike, her husband Moishe and their infant son Irving lived in New York. Moishe ran a laundromat while Chaike worked in a clothing factory. They had a hard life. When Moishe heard about Motl's dealings with Arke he felt that he, a Talmud scholar and actor and a more mature person than Motl, would be able to explain matters to Arke and come to an agreement with him. And so, without consulting Motl, he and Chaike sold the laundromat, bought a nice new car, a Hudson, and moved to Chaike's hometown of Montreal. At first all was well between them and Odel and Arke. They even rented a summer house together in the Laurentians and invited Chienke and the children to visit for a while. But it didn't take long for Chaike and Moishe to realize their mistake. When their plans fell through they had to rely on Motl's parents and on Motl and Chienke for help. The two cousins, Yankale and Itzikel (Irving), who became lifelong friends, were the only winners in this venture. After two years of struggle, Chaike and Moishe sold their car and moved back to the United States. This time they went to Detroit where Moishe bought another laundromat and Chaike worked in another factory.

Yet another opportunity developed when Motl read an ad in the newspaper from a war veteran who was looking for a partner with knowledge of the building trade and who would be willing to invest $10,000 in a building project on the outskirts of Montreal. Motl was interested. He called the veteran and arranged a visit to his home in a veteran's housing project near the Canadair factory. The veteran had no money; he had only his plans and his carpenter's tools. The idea involved buying a nearby plot of land, building a model house and then building additional houses for buyers using low interest (2%) government mortgages. The proposal sounded very good. However, when Motl and Chienke thought it over they realized that while the project would generate large profits if it was successful, if it failed Motl would be the loser. They were afraid to take the risk.

Motl's work and responsibilities expanded two-fold during the post-war period. Part-time help was no longer adequate. He needed a full-time assistant, someone to work at night to clean the 16 classrooms that were used for the day school and for classes held in the afternoons.

The Adath Israel became an even more active centre of Jewish life. The struggle for Jewish statehood in *Eretz Yisrael* had a deep influence in and around the congregation. At the same time, the first survivors of the Holocaust began to appear. At first, they tended to live in the old Jewish neighborhood in downtown Montreal. Later, when more Jewish families moved to the outlying suburbs, the new arrivals could move into apartments located near the synagogue. Motl and Chienke befriended them and helped them find employment. In time they settled in to their new lives and, in some cases became prosperous.

The educational activities in Adath Israel kept expanding and in no time even the classrooms in the new extension were fully occupied. The post-war prosperity, along with a post-Holocaust increase in Jewish awareness, led to an intense interest in Jewish education. Under the president's leadership, and with the support of the Zionist-oriented membership and the Rabbi and Principal, a decision to build a Hebrew high school was made. The addition would be built on an empty lot across the street on Ducharme, on land purchased from the City of Outremont.

The new addition would take some time to build and in the meantime there was no room for the expanded kindergarten. It was decided that the superintendent's apartment could be used, as a temporary location. This time an apartment was rented nearby on Ducharme Street and Motl and his family could enjoy privacy once again.

By this time, Miriam (Mirale) was about to graduate from Strathcona Academy, while Yankale was six years old and attending Hebrew day school. Motl's sister Rochel encouraged Chienke to become involved in the *Naamat* woman's organization. Chienke and the children spent summers in a rented country house in Piedmont in the Laurentians north of Montreal, while Motl joined them on weekends. Chienke's brother Itzel also joined them, as did Motl's parents who were driven up for their first summer holiday by Motl's brother Hershel. During the days they walked around and breathed the fresh air while in the evenings the older couple could enjoy their grandchildren and they, in turn, could listen to their *Zaide* as he read from his memoirs. It was a time to remember

Now we'll go back to the situation during the early years of Adath Israel Congregation. When the sanctuary first began to function in 1941, a cantor was hired to conduct the High Holiday services. The cantor was a bearded man from England, a survivor of the blitz, who charged a high price for his services. This cantor sang as loudly as possible, as if to prove his worth. The people praying felt sorry for him, especially the women, so the synagogue officials told him, "We will pay you regardless, but please don't pray so loudly!"

The next year the congregation made do without a special High Holidays cantor because of the war. The Rabbi himself performed the *Mussaf* prayers. However, in the following year, another cantor, a refugee from Germany with an operatic voice, was hired. This cantor was Motl and Chienke's age. In Germany he had belonged to the *Hechalutz* movement and so he had a lot in common with Motl and Chienke and they became friends. Once, just before *Kol Nidre* on the eve of Yom Kippur, Chienke noticed that he was wearing leather shoes instead of slippers. She asked, "Don't you know that as a representative of the congregation before God you should not wear leather shoes?" He tried on Motl's slippers but they were too small. Since leather shoes are not worn on Yom Kippur because leather was traditionally associated with wealth and comfort, he had to perform the *Kol Nidre* service in his stockings. Later he became a cantor for a reform temple in New York and still later he sang opera at the Metropolitan.

All in all, the congregation was disappointed with the cantors who were stars. Two years after the war they hired a traditional cantor who was well known in the old country, the town of Uman in the Ukraine. As he was a friend of Motl's father from yeshiva days, Motl's parents decided to join their children for the High Holidays in order to enjoy his praying. In fact, everybody felt nostalgic as they listened to him. He was old and his voice was not as strong as it used to be, but his interpretive abilities made up for it. This was when Motl and his family were already living in the new extension. Chienke gave the beds to the older couple while she and Motl and Mirale slept on the floor. Motl's parents could see how hard their son worked to make a living.

While Motl's parents were 75 years old they still attended to their grocery store. This was because Freide, Motl's mother, considered that any social assistance was charity. As a result, they were not receiving the monthly federal old age pension of forty dollars that they were entitled to. But while vacationing in Piedmont with Chienke and Motl she noticed how Motl turned the children's allowance cheques he had received over to Chienke. Chienke explained that it was not charity but rather money owed them for their work by the government. At this point, Freide stopped objecting and

Reb David applied for a pension. Elderly Jews normally went to the Baron de Hirshe office for assistance with the application. However, when they got to the office, after closing their grocery for a day, they found a long waiting line. They found that they might have to wait for weeks and that the office staff was rude and offhand. Reb David stood up and went home with Freide, angry and disappointed. They called their son Motl and asked him what they should do. Motl went to the principal of the Adath Israel School and told him the story and together they told the Rabbi. The Rabbi picked up the telephone and immediatly called the Baron de Hirshe office. He said, "This is the Rabbi speaking. My good friends David and Freide Sivak need to fill out their old age pension applications and they will be at the office in the morning. Attend to them right away and see that the matter is taken care of!" And it was taken care of.

Then there was the problem of disposing of the grocery store. Motl's father was not interested in selling it for a profit and in any case who would want a store in the older Jewish section of Montreal? Perhaps one of the new arrivals who had survived the Holocaust would be interested? Instead, he insisted that every item in the store be sold for its cost value. Motl was too busy to deal with this situation but fortunately Rochel and Hershel took care of it and their parent's move to another house in the same building.

Part 3: Mirale and Yankale

During this period, Mirale graduated from the Hebrew afternoon school. At that time there was no Hebrew high school and so she attended Strathcona Academy. However, her graduation from the afternoon school became controversial over the issue of who would get the prize as best student. In fact, Mirale was the best, but the Rabbi was concerned that the close friendship between Motl and Chienke and the teachers (some were old friends from the Zionist youth movement) might appear to have influenced the decision. It was rumored that another girl would be given the prize. When one of Mirale's classmates came by to visit, Chienke asked her who she thought would get the prize. She anwered, "Miriam of course."

Chienke decided to do something about this situation. She did not want Mirale to lose faith in society. After she approached the principal, the Rabbi and the president, both girls were awarded the first prize.

In the meantime, Yankale began studies in the Hebrew day school. One day, after he had begun to learn *chumash*[36] he came home crying bitterly. Motl and Chienke asked what had happened, "Did you fall and hurt yourself?" "No," he said, "But how can brothers throw one of them into a pit to be devoured by wild beasts?" Then Chienke understood that he was upset by the story of Joseph and his brothers. Motl tried to explain that the story had taken place 3000 years ago. When Motl met the teacher he asked, "Why did you frighten my son?" The teacher replied, "This is how we teach that the Torah is alive today."

Another story about Yankale concerns the period when he was a student in the Hebrew high school and Motl was in business on his own. One of the teachers called Motl and Chienke to tell them about a composition that Yankale had written, in which he described his family, a family in which the parents helped each other in their affairs and how his sister was studying to be a chartered accountant and and how she had married a meteorologist, and so-on.

A Hebrew Academy (the new high school) was completed in 1951. It was an impressive structure but too expensive and not revenue-generating. It was too much for one office girl. An executive level administrator, a man, was hired to oversee the many operations of the synagogue. The administrator decided that he would take over all matters pertaining to the various supplies that were used. Until then, school supplies and books were dealt with by the principal, and he and the Rabbi were glad to turn it all over to the new man. But when Motl was asked to relinquish his control over maintenance supplies he refused. The matter was brought to the attention of the

---

[36] Bible.

Board of Directors. They called Motl in to a meeting and asked why he did not cooperate with the new administrator. Motl gave them the same answer that he gave years earlier: "When I drive the car, I myself handle the steering wheel." The board members were astonished at Chienke's Motl's *chutzpah*!

At this time the president of the synagogue was not friendly to Motl and his family. The high school was complete and the superintendent's apartment was rennovated and ready for occupancy. The synagogue's expenses were increasing while its revenues were going down. Wealthier members were moving away to the suburbs. Motl was asked to move back into the synagogue to save the rent for his apartment. He was also asked to give up the checking room concession. But Mirale was by then a student at McGill University and it was time for Motl's family to have a normal private life. Motl was willing to continue in his job but he needed to keep the checking room concession. The number of functions in the two halls was decreasing because of new synagogues in the suburbs, and he was worried about his income.

In the summer of 1951 the new administrator was dismissed because of a costly error. A new administrator, an honest man with a Zionist youth background, was hired to replace him. A new bookkeeper, a traditional Jew from Czechoslovakia who had survived the Holocaust, was hired as well. Motl developed a close and trusting relationship with both of them. That summer Motl enjoyed the house in the country.

The synagogue sanctuary needed to be renovated but the decision to start the job was made too late. Now the High Holidays were about to begin and the job was not finished. The income from the High Holiday services was crucial to the synagogue. To speed the contractor's work Motl hired extra assistants to help with the cleaning up. The president came by and noticed all the workers. Realizing that this was costing the synagogue money, he began to give orders to the assistants to work faster, all the while ignoring Motl. Motl could see that if the president continued to interfere by ordering the workers around they would stop listening to Motl and the job would never get done. Motl went over to the president and said, "If you think you can do a better job as superintendent, here are the keys." This was the beginning of Motl's decision to leave the synagogue.

A new man, a Holocaust survivor with a wife and two children, was hired to be the superintendent. He agreed to live in the synagogue and, as he was observant, he also did the job of assistant shamas (sextant). In addition, he agreed to give up the checking room concession. Of course, instead, he insisted on being tipped by the parents of the bride and groom, by the musicians, the bartenders, the florists, and so on.

The new superintendent moved in at the beginning of 1952 but the synagogue asked Motl to stay on the job until June in order to help the new man get organized. In return, the congregation promised to continue paying Motl's salary and the rent for his apartment until August. Chienke's Motl really deserved more, especially as he was leaving the synagogue and wasn't being asked to leave. But, he accepted the arrangements and his goodwill was rewarded, for the synagogue officials told him that when it came time for a wedding for Mirale and a bar mitzvah for Yankale they would be delighted if they were celebrated in Adath Israel and there would be no charge.

The winter passed and it was already Purim. On Purim it had become a tradition that, in addition to morning services and the megilla reading at night, there would be a Purim carnival for the schoolchildren and a Purim dinner for the congregation. All year long Motl had said that the carnival should be held on one day and the dinner on the next. But the Rabbi and the principal decided not to pay attention to Motl, who was leaving anyway, and arranged both events for the same day. Motl could have brought the matter to the attention of the administration, but he did not want to cause trouble for the Rabbi or the principal. Motl got the new superintendent and the assistants together with the necessary cleaning materials as soon as the carnival ended at four o'clock. The dinner was to begin at six o'clock. The two halls were a terrible mess and when the arrangements committee saw the mess they angrily asked Motl about it. He told them to ask the Rabbi and the principal: "But for the meantime just wait and see." Motl began to direct the clean-up and before the six o'clock deadline the rooms were transformed into the equivalent of hotel ballrooms. The members of the arrangements committee thanked Motl and shook his hand. "Now," they said, "we really understand what you have meant to our synagogue all these years."

While Motl was still working at the Adath Israel, during the last six months, he began to worry about the future. He and Chienke knew a couple from their youth who owned a stationary store on Van Horne Street, near the synagogue. One day when Motl was visiting the store his friend told him that he was planning to rent the adjacent store and sell toys. He felt that Motl could help run the two businesses. If Motl had $10,000 to invest they could become partners. Chienke thought it was a good idea. All that was needed was to go to a notary and sign a partnership agreement. The friend was a busy man but in the meantime Motl spent some time in the store to become acquainted with his future business. Motl made an effort to reorganize the store to improve efficiency. Suddenly, however, the friend approached Motl and told him that his uncle advised him to conduct his business by himself, without a partner! Fortunately, Motl and Chienke still had the $10,000; they wouldn't have turned it over before signing a legal contract. Now, however, they would have to struggle to find a new way to make a living. They accepted the challenge with the same spirit that they had when they left the kibbutz. This time it would be easier. They had $13,000 in savings, a very large sum, to Chienke and Motl.

To complete this chapter on the Adath Israel, we will turn to Mirale's wedding, which took place a year after Motl left his job at the synagogue and to Yankale's bar mitzvah three years after that. Mirale's wedding was a very happy occasion. There was a lot of singing and dancing with a large number of young people and the whole family, including Bubbe Freide and Zaide David, was there. However, Zaide passed away before Yankale's bar mitzvah, and Bubbe was sick and could not attend; nor could Chienke's eldest sister Leah, who was in the hospital. Leah and her husband Meir were responsible for teaching Yankale how to chant the *haftorah*, and he did an excellent job. The members of the congrgation who were there congratulated Chienke and Motl and said that they were proud of him and the fact that he had been born in their shul. The Rabbi made a presentation and said some words about Motl and Chienke and how they had been *chalutzim* not only *in Eretz Yisrael* but also in the Adath Israel.

Now we can ask what has become of this once important institution? The Rabbi and the cantor and the president and the principal are no longer alive. The sanctuary and the extension attached to it were sold and have become a Lebanese Christian church. The high shool has been taken over by a chassidic organization as a school for girls. Yes, there is a new Adath Israel synagogue in a now affluent Jewish neighborhood in the town of Hampstead. But now it is just a modern orthodox synagogue. There is no community centre, no school and no Jewish superintendent is living there. The idea that led to the development of the original Adath Israel, with its emphasis on intensive Jewish education, was not passed on. Too bad.

Jacob's Commentary

In the forword, I mentioned briefly that I spent the early years of my life living with my parents and sister in an apartment located in the synagogue/Hebrew school complex known as Adath Israel. The word *Adath*, by the way, refers to an assembly or congregation. I have no memory of the original apartment that existed before the expansion, referred to by my father. But I do remember the aprtment we lived in at Hampstead on an interim basis for 18 months and the new synagogue apartment that we moved back to and lived in until I was seven years old.

The Adath Israel apartment was located at ground level in the new wing constructed to create a Jewish elementary parochial school. Instruction was in English and Hebrew on a 50/50 basis and French language classes commenced in the middle of grade three. (Unfortunately, I was away for a few weeks with something like the mumps or chicken pox at the start of French instruction and as a result, French was the bane of my existence for a long time. Many years later whan I was in high school an excellent teacher straightened me out and French became one of my strong subjects)

To get back to the apartment, I can only recall two bedrooms and so I must have shared a room with my sister. The entrance to the apartment was next to a large entrance foyer to the new wing, which led to a large assembly hall. All grade school students assembled in this hall every morning. We sang the Jewish (now also the Israeli) anthem, *Hatikvah* and then *Oh Canada*, before marching off to our classes, two-by-two. I also recall singing *God Save the King* on one ocassion, the death of King George VI in 1952. The assembly hall was also used as a play area at recess and as a lunchroom at noon. It was converted into a temporary scanctuary for services during the High Holidays in the fall. The door to the apartment was located opposite the stairway that led to the three floors of classrooms located above the hall. As a toddler, I was able to roam around various parts of the building, particularly in the early evening when the cleaners opened all the offices doors in order to do their job. The office of Mr. Mendelsohn, the principal, contained a number of souvenirs and artifacts from the Holy Land that were of particular interest to a little boy. On one occasion I pressed a button located beside his desk and it wasn't long before police and fire sirens could be heard on their way to see to a possible emergency. I disappeared well before anyone could put two and two together.

Living in the synagogue was, I now realize, a unique experience. However, at the time I know that I didn't think it was unusual at all. Living in the synagogue meant that I was somewhat isolated as far as friends my own age were concerned. Many of my memories of that period concern the various workers my father hired to help cater the numerous functions that took place as well as to help with the logistics of High Holiday services in the fall. I remember Mike, who my father refers to, was a kindly man who built a birdhouse for me from two rectangular cigar boxes. He was a heavy smoker and I remember his nicotine-stained fingers. At that time I guess filter cigarettes were not common and Mike would smoke his down to the last few millimeters. I also have very fond memories of the Slovaks, the two Annies and Mary and George. One individual who stands out was a Russian named Fiodor, who was a very tall man, at least in my eyes. He had a scar on one cheek and I can recall watching him eat a dozen boiled eggs for lunch.

One of the principal caterers involved in providing food for the weddings and other affairs was Mrs Zatz. Mrs Zatz had a grandson, Ian, who often came with her, along with his mother who also worked as a caterer. Ian and I were given treats to eat from the leftovers. In particular, I remember eating some wonderful oven-roasted chicken wings. A type of sorbet dessert in the shape of strawberries, which were referred to as "ices", was another favourite. I was given to understand that Ian's father was in the hospital, and Ian showed me a get well letter he was writing to his father. When I was several years older and could read the newspaper I found out that Ian's father was actually in prison for a gangland slaying that took place in the late 1940s, when Montreal was one of the vice capitals of North America. The newspaper item referred to his parole after a successful appeal of his sentence on the basis of self-defense.

One of my memories of this period of my life was an evening, probably in 1949, shortly after the establishment of the State of Israel, when I was able to see and listen to a concert given in the synagogue hall by Shoshana Damari, a popular Israeli singer who was to become a cultural icon. My mother loved her songs and would sing a number of them, particularly when I was younger and when her (my mother's) voice was better than it was later in her life. Of course her favorite was Damari's signature song "Kalaniot," recorded in 1948. The song is about a little girl who dreams about gathering anemones (flowers) for her mother but a common interpretation is the flowers of the song were intended to be a code to alert pre-state Jewish forces as to the presence of British soldiers, the red flowers symbolizing their red caps.

In this chapter, my father refers to his decision to leave the synagogue and his effort to buy into an exisiting store that was located on a street near the Adath Israel complex. The store was a newsstand and stationary store and the owner, who was referred to as Harry Buckingham because of a large advertisement above the door for Buckingham cigarettes, was taking over the store next door and wanted to expand his business to include a toy store. My father would get his daily Yiddish newspaper, either *Der Tog* (The Day) or *Der Forverts*, from this store. My parents had saved the grand sum of $13,000 during their years of work for the synagogue. The money was essentially the tips from the coat and hat checking concession that my father referred to earlier. I can remember helping my mother organizing the pennies into rolls that could be deposited in the bank. To my parents it was an enormous sum of money, and a critically important cushion at a time when there was no government health insurance. Moreover, my father's job at the synagogue did not include a pension plan. The money was to be used in the transition from the job at Adath Israel to a new form of livelihood. All their hopes rested with the partnership that was arranged with Harry. When he let them down, my parents had to cast about for something else and that led to the installment merchant business described in the next chapter. My father never forgave Harry for his change of heart and never set foot in his store again. From then on he purchased his Yiddish daily newspaper from a store located two blocks away.

Retrospective

Before actually getting into Chapter 7, my father thought it best to review the topics he had covered in the earlier 6 chapters as well as the topics that were to come. As can be seen from the list that appears below, his intent was to produce a description of his entire life. He felt that each phase of his life involved a struggle and that each struggle required the same pioneering approach so well embodied in the Hebrew phrase, "chazak v'amatz", be strong and be brave. However, as I indicated in the foreword, the more recent events described were ones that I could remember as well and as a result they were not as interesting to me. My father also lost interest in continuing the translating effort once he felt that the key events of his life had been documented. He did translate Chapters 8 and 9. These deal mainly with family matters and my parents' Zionist activities in their waning years. While I have kept the translations my father made of these two chapters, I decided to stop after number 7 and my father didn't object. However, the entire list as he intended is intact below. As is the case for the earlier chapters, my own thoughts and views appear at the end of the chapter describing how my father became an installment merchant.

The first two chapters describe Motl and Chienke's childhoods; how they grew up in their respective shtetels in the Ukraine and in Lithuania. Motl's experience as a refugee for three years in Kishenev, Moldavia, and his early involvement in the Jewish scout movement, *Hashomer Hatzair*, are dealt with in the first chapter while Chienke's childhood is described in the second one.

In chapter three, Motl and Chienke are involved in various youth movements in Montreal: *Hashomer Hatzair*, *Poale Zion* and *Hechalutz*. Motl's trip to western Canada, family developments and general events in Jewish life are described.

Chapter four starts first with Motl's *Aliyah* to Palestine. Later, he is joined by Chienke as they experience kibbutz life together. By Chapter five, they are disappointed and have left the kibbutz to struggle for one more year in Palestine before returning to Canada to visit Motl's parents. The struggle to survive economically continues until the outbreak of World War II.

Chapter six deals with Chienke and Motl's thirteen years of work, and living in the Adath Israel Congregation and Hebrew school (afternoon school, day school and high school academy) and community center.

After a delay in the translation of these memoirs from Yiddish to English, caused by Chienke's illness and death, Motl continued the translation of the next three chapters.

Chapter seven describes how, at the age of 42, Motl, the former *chalutz* and pioneer, becam an installment merchant, struggling to fit into a new role and having interesting experiences.

Chapters eight and nine describe family events, both the happy occasions as well as the tragic ones, the family problems, and Chinke's and Motl's social lives and organizational work, Motl in the Farband Labor Zionist Alliance and Chienke in the Naamat Pioneer Women organization. Together they participated in the General Zionist Moment and the Canadian Jewish Congress.

The last three chapters (ten, eleven and twelve) were not translated. Chapter ten is devoted to the the education of their children, Miriam and Jacob, family summers in the Laurentians, a New Year's trip to New York City and summer trips to Old Orchard Beach, Saratoga Springs, Atlantic City and Bethlehem, Vermont.

In chapter eleven, Motl retires at age 75 and winters are spent in Miami Beach. Motl and Chienke also visit Israel, more than once, and both are active socially in Montreal.

Finally, Chapter twelve, old age: Chienke's illness and death, the continuation of Motl's work and concern for an enlightened secular Jewish life in Yiddish, Hebrew and other languages.

Chapter 7: How Chienke's Motl Became an Installment Merchant

In June, 1952 Motl stopped working for the Adath Israel Congregation. He left with a record of devotion to the institution and for that he was given three extra months' salary and three months' rent for his apartment. He was also reminded that Adath Israel would be honoured to be the site of Mirale's wedding and Yankale's bar mitzvah.

But how was the family going to make a living? Motl and Chienke were 42, Miriam was 18 and a student at McGill University, and Jacob was 8 and a student in the Adath Israel elementary parochial school.

At this point, Motl's proletarian dreams were meaningless, particularly in the context of the post-war period. Motl's family and friends advised him to purchase a retail business, as was the common Jewish way. This was not in Motl and Chienke's thinking, nor did they have the money. While they had saved $13,000 during the thirteen years that they worked for the *shul*, and while this was a large sum of money to them, it was not enough to buy a business.

So Motl's sister, Rochel, advised him to learn how to become an installment merchant (or customer peddler). Motl turned for help to Rochel's friend David, who was a successful installment merchant, for help. David helped Motl make contact with Oscar, a dry goods wholesaler on Main Street (St. Laurent). David sympathized with Motl for he too had pioneering dreams in his youth but they never materialized. With a salute of *chazak ve'amatz* he wished Motl luck in the new business.

What sort of business was it? Well, it began at the start of the century when newly-arrived Jewish immigrants without cash turned to peddlers, to buy goods on credit or term payments. In time, the business became concentrated in the poor working class French Canadian districts of Montreal, where the concept of banking and saving a part of one's salary was not common. When a need to buy a substantial item arose they never had the cash, and the large businesses did not extend credit. Jewish business filled this need, in realizing that ordinary people were trustworthy. By adding a surcharge for the goods, everyone was happy. The customer had what he wanted and the salesman made his profit. In more recent times, the large business enterprises also began to understand that giving credit to ordinary working people was worthwhile, and the credit card was born.

Oscar, the dry goods wholesaler, helped Motl get started. First he told Motl to buy a good working car. Then, he, Oscar, would prepare packages containing pillows, pillowcases, sheets, blankets and bed covers. Motl would pay $27 for each package and charge $50 (plus $3 tax) to be paid out on the basis of $1 per week. He advised Motl to pick a likely location and then knock on doors to make sales. Each sale would help create a customer for other household needs.

Motl bought a car, a Plymouth, for $2,500 and four parcels from Oscar. Oscar wished him luck and Motl went off wondering what would come next. On the following Tuesday, a lucky day, Motl knocked on the first door. It was opened by a man still in his pyjamas. When Motl offered his merchandise, he was invited in to meet his sympathetic wife. Mr. And Mrs. Bouchard were newlyweds who had just returned from their honeymoon to an empty house. Motl could see that they slept on rags on the floor. To them the parcel of goods was heaven-sent. Mr. Bouchard agreed to the charge of $53 and gave Motl a down payment of $5. He offered to pay Motl $5 per week. One dollar was not enough, as he and his wife would be ordering more items in the weeks ahead.

After Motl was invited to have a cup of coffee, he felt brave enough to ask Mr. Bouchard if he could introduce him to neighbors and friends who might also need his merchandise. At this point, Mr. Bouchard got dressed and took Motl to visit some neighbors. Motl sold the other three parcels in short order to the Houles, the Gariepys and the Davies. They all agreed to the terms and gave him down payments.

When Motl arrived home early, well before noon, Chienke wondered what had happened. But when Motl showed her the signed contracts and the down payments she began to realize that she had been hasty in thinking that her former *chalutz* would not be able to do this kind of business. She served Motl a nourishing meal and told him to take the rest of the day off. But Motl went back to a surprised Oscar for four new parcels that day. When Motl showed Oscar the contracts, Oscar told him that he would make a good businessman but he warned him that it wouldn't always be so easy.

The very next day, Motl knocked on a door on a street next to the one on which he had been so lucky. This time the door was half opened by a strange looking woman who demanded to know what he wanted. Motl tried to explain but the woman cursed and slammed the door.

Motl was shaken by the experience and could not continue. He returned home to Chienke, convinced that he would not be able to knock on strange doors any more. Chienke ran downstairs to their good neighbors, Sylvia and Meyer, for help and advice. Meyer, a businessman himself, told Motl that he did not need to sell parcels door-to-door to find customers. He promised to introduce Motl to relatives of his who developed an electric appliance company. They would sell their products to Motl at wholesale prices and with three months credit. Motl would have to canvass potential customers. Motl received the same response from friendly members of Adath Israel who were involved in the manufacture of furniture and men's and lady's clothing.

With this encouragement, Motl began to call friends and colleagues who had worked with him over the years at the *shul*. These included waiters and waitresses, bartenders, photographers, musicians and so on. Motl had always treated them very fairly and they were pleased to hear from him. When he described his new business, many became his customers, some on credit terms and some on the basis of cash sales. With these contacts Motl was able to get his business started.

Some family members went out of their way to help Motl get started in business. His parents were able to get him customers from the people they knew on their street. Itzel, Chienke's brother, who was a sick man, knew another customer peddler who wanted to sell some accounts. Motl bought 25 of them at a reasonable cost and these remained good clients for the duration of Motl's business activity. Chienke's sisters, Leah and Rivka, two well-qualified Hebrew teachers, were devoted to their younger sister's family. When a domestic, a Ukrainian woman, asked where they bought their furniture, she was told about their brother-in-law. The woman told Motl that she and a neighbor each needed a house full of furniture but that Saturday was the only time that they were free. So Motl organized all the necessary appointments in advance and on Saturday he sold $4,000 worth of furniture to the first woman and then $3,500 to her neighbor. The first sale included a down payment of $400 and monthly payments of $50 while the second involved monthly payments of $40. At the end of that day Motl and Chienke visited his parents as they did every Saturday evening, and Motl felt that he had shown that he was capable of being a success in business.

When he established himself, Motl's enterprise included 150 paying accounts. It is worth introducing a few of the special customers and characters that Chienke and Motl had to interact with during this period in their lives.

For thirty years, Motl, the installment merchant, wandered the streets of Montreal and its suburbs, driving ten different cars, mostly Plymouths and Ford Customs, as he served nearly 400 different customers representing a wide range of ethnic groups, although most were French Canadians.

Mr. Bouchard, the first customer, continued buying from Motl for a few years until he didn't need any more credit. After the last payment, Motl joked to Mrs. Bouchard that he would miss his visits to her home. She took him seriously and told Motl to keep to his weekly schedule. Instead of payments, she would continue to give Motl $5 a week as a form of savings. So Motl continued to visit for a few weeks until the more level headed Mr. Bouchard told Motl that he would rather use a bank to deposit their savings, but that he would continue to recommend customers, which in fact he did.

Mr. And Mrs. Newman, Hungarian survivors of the Holocaust, moved to a flat across the street from Motl's parents. Mr. Newman had a job in the needle trade but their house was empty of furnishings. When Motl's parents were asked for advice they told the Newmans not to worry, their son Motl would help them find what they needed on reasonable credit terms. And that is what happened. Many years later, when Motl was much older, he went to a modern synagogue in Cote St. Luc to hear Yitzchak Shamir, the ex-prime minister of Israel, speak. The hall was full and there did not appear to be any empty seats. Suddenly, Mr. Newman appeared. He was well off and one of the important figures in the synagogue. Motl was given a special seat at the front with all the notables who were attending.

The Dions were customers who Motl canvassed, himself, one day when he approached two women playing cards and asked if they needed a parcel of bed linens. One of them introduced herself as Mrs. Dion and pointed to a bare bed. She took a package but told Motl to come by on Friday evenings when her husband would pay him. When Motl came back on Friday evenings, he found a man sitting at the kitchen table in front of two large bottles of beer, one being half empty. When Motl asked if he was Mr. Dion, the drunken man said that he was. But when Motl gave him the bill for the package of bedding that his wife bought, the man told him that he had no wife! Motl said, "But you have the linens and the woman said that you would make the payments." The man replied that the woman had slept with him for a couple of nights but now she was gone and he wanted Motl to take the goods back. Motl told him that if he took the goods back they would be useless and the bed would be bare again. The drunken man looked at Motl and said that he needed a trench coat. If he could get one on the next day, Saturday, he would keep the linen, give Motl a down payment of $10 and payments of $5 per week. Motl had to agree. Now he had a client who paid him $5 weekly instead of $1!

This arrangement went on for some time until one Friday Motl arrived to find an empty house. Luckily, Motl had noted on a card that Mr. Dion worked for the Vickers shipbuilding company. On Monday Chienke bravely telephoned the Vickers office and asked to speak to Mr. Dion. When she was told that he was at a meeting, she left her number and asked that he call back. That night, he called and apologized. For various reasons he had had to move, and he provided his new address. Motl continued to come by every week, but now there were new purchases and the weekly payments were $10.

What was Mr. Dion's problem? He was the son of middle-class French Canadian parents and a successful electrical engineer. But with no family and no social life, his only interest was in his professional work during the week. On Friday after work he ordered two dozen large bottles of beer and, keeping two bottles at a time on the kitchen table, he drank through the weekend. When Motl asked why he always kept two bottles on the table, he answered that he needed the stimulation of seeing the next full bottle.

Mr. Dion continued to make new purchases, so the account and the weekly payments kept getting larger. When Motl asked why he needed to buy on credit, he said that at least this way someone comes to visit him once a week and, besides, he enjoyed his conversations with Motl.

This went on for a couple of years, until Motl discovered that Mr. Dion had passed away. Motl was sorry of course, but he also worried about the $1500 balance in his account. But there was no need to worry as Mr. Dion's will made sure that Motl was paid in full.

The Breux family represented another interesting experience for Motl and Chienke. They were one of the accounts that Itzel recommended. Chienke referred to them as the Plouffe family, after the popular Quebecois television series of that name. Mr. Breux was an army veteran who became a milk truck driver. Mrs. Breux really looked like the Mrs. Plouffe of television. They were descendents of early French Canadian settlers and they lived on St. Timothy Street in the downtown slum district of Montreal. They were content with their lifestyle. When Motl mentioned to Mr. Breux that as a veteran he was entitled to buy a house in a newer part of town at a low interest of only 2%, he looked at Motl with astonishment. He said, "Why do I have to buy a house when I can pay rent and it is as if it is my house?"

Mr. Breux was always happy. He had a voice like that of an opera singer and he and his wife had many children. Some were orphans or abandoned children that they took care of. They bought from Motl for many years and they kept on referring customers to him. To them it was a pleasure.

One Friday night Motl found Mrs. Breux crying. When he asked what happened, she told him that her husband was robbed of his week's salary on his way to a tavern after work. "How will I manage during the coming week?" she asked. So Motl advanced her $10 on her account and she felt better. In time, the whole family and their neighbours became customers of Motl's.

By the time Motl retired, the Breux family had changed. Their grandchildren were well educated and may have been involved in the separatist movement. They didn't need to buy on credit anymore. Motl and Chienke had fond memories of them as good common people.

Mrs. Metcalf was a waitress who often worked in the Adath Israel. She was always friendly with Chienke and Motl. Although she was a gentile, she lived in an old Jewish neighborhood on Colonial Street, between Pine and Prince Arthur. Her children could even speak a little Yiddish and when they grew up they married into a variety of ethnic groups, including Jews. When Motl called her to tell her about his new business, she invited him to come over as she and her many children needed to buy on credit.

Her next-door-neighbor, Mrs. Alie, was another interesting customer. She was an orphan who was raised in a convent under strict disciplinary conditions. When she grew up she became a piano player working in nightclubs as well as a free thinker and a radical. She was a tall, impressive woman who had a number of love affairs with a variety of men, including Jewish ones. She gave birth to many children, and she kept in touch with the various men who were a part of her life. In time, her lovers and, as they grew up, her children, also became Motl's customers.

As time went on, Mrs. Alie and her lovers died and her children moved away to different cities. One Saturday night, when Chienke and Motl were already living in Chomedy, and Motl was having a game of chess with his good friend Mr. Hendler, there was a knock on the door. It was Robert, Mrs. Alie's youngest son. Motl invited him in and Chienke served refreshments. Robert told them the reason for his sudden visit. He had become a taxi driver and had been given a $100 traffic ticket. He had nobody to turn to but Motl and if he did not pay the $100 he would have to go to jail. So Motl and Chienke lent him the money. Mr. Hendler was sure that they would never see the money again, but Robert paid them back and went on to become a good customer.

To describe all of the many customers Motl had to deal with is not possible. So, we'll finish this chapter with a look at the Briere family. Mr. Briere was a hard-working truck driver who worked double shifts. He and his family lived in a wooden shack of a house on a muddy street in Montreal North. In winter, the snow blew into the house through cracks in the walls and the house was largely unfurnished. Mrs. Briere was from a North American Indian background. Their many children played and slept on rags. They told Motl that they needed everything, from A to Z.

In one year, the Brieres' account with Motl totalled more then $2000 and they were making weekly payments of $15. Still, Mr. Briere wanted Motl to sell him a television set. Motl resisted. He didn't think they could afford it. Mr. Briere pleaded and offered to pay $20 a week but Motl wouldn't give in. The next Saturday, when Motl came for his weekly collection, a well-dressed salesman from a furniture company, a Jew, was sitting at the table writing out a contract for a television. He asked Mr. Briere for the names and addresses of references. This was something new for Mr. Briere. Motl had trusted him and never asked for references. He grew angry and, grabbing the well-dressed gentleman by the neck, threw him out of the house into the snow. Then he turned to Motl said, "I can do business with you. You trust me. Sell me a television set and I'll pay you $20 a week." So, Motl had no alternative but to sell him a television.

Motl's contract with the Brieres went on for some time until one day he came and found that their house had been demolished! It took Motl some time to find them for they had moved a considerable distance away to live with their immediate families. When Motl arrived at their new place, Mr. Briere apologized and promised to pay

Motl regularly. Motl insisted that because of the distance he would have to be paid by mail or with post-dated checques. But Mr. Briere pleaded with Motl that he did not know how to save money or deal with banks, and so Motl had to teach him how to save and how to use a bank and finally Mr. Briere paid him with post-dated cheques so that Motl was able to collect, even when he and Cheinke were away for the winter.

This chapter deals with an important part of Motl and Chienke's lives in terms of how they made a living. While this was going on, there were a number of family events, some happy and some tragic, as well as social and political happenings in Montreal and elsewhere.

Jacob's Commentary

My father's work as an installment merchant took place during most of the formative years of my life, beginning when I was about eight years old and extending until after my marriage and the year (1968) my wife and I left Montreal. During this period I had many opportunities to be with my parents, or sometimes only with my father, as he took care of his business.

The first and obvious change in our lives was the acquisition of our first car, a green 1952 Plymouth that was used for recreational purposes as well as for business. With the car, my parents and I were able to undertake a number of motoring trips to such destinations as Ottawa, Quebec City and Old Orchard Beach, Maine. My sister was almost 10 years older than I and married when she was 19 years old, as was customary. As a result, I usually travelled with my parents by myself, except for the trip to Quebec City when one of my friends, Lionel, was invited along to keep me company.

My role during these road trips was to act as navigator since map reading was not something my mother could deal with, and she never drove. My father was a terrible driver who was never able to learn many of the skills that are associated with good driving habits.

For example, he never used the rear view mirror (side placed mirrors were rare or non-existent at that time) and so when he changed lanes he just gradually and slowly moved over, giving the following drivers time to adjust. While he did have accidents from time to time, these were generally minor in nature since he drove very, very slowly. I recall a drive to Gloversville, New York to visit family, a town only 170 miles or so from Montreal. While it is true that this trip took place before the existence of the throughway that exists today, it should not have taken the 12 hours or so that I recall, even with the stop we made to see Ausable Chasm on the way.

The possession of a car and the mobility it provided also gave my father an opportunity to look up old friends from his Zionist youth. He had an uncanny ability to track them down after decades had elapsed and even after their names had been changed. This happened on trips to Ottawa, Toronto, Niagara Falls, and New York City. It usually meant that I would be in for a boring visit to a stranger's home while my father and his rediscovered friends reminisced and became caught up on the latest news

In addition to the many road trips away from Montreal, I spent many days driving all over Montreal as my father conducted business, and while he was a terrible driver, my father had an excellent sense of direction and could navigate the complex of urban streets with ease. Most of his time involved collecting money, usually on a weekly or monthly basis, from his many customers. The amount varied, depending on the size of the amount owed, but it could be as little as one dollar. My father had long cards for each customer with his own name imprinted at the top and a series of horizontal lines so he could indicate the date, the amount collected and the balance owed.

My father used a variety of wholesalers to service his costumers' needs. When it came to clothing, his primary resource was Brown's Department Store, a retail/wholesale store on St Laurent Street. Another one, used less extensively, was Montreal Outfitters, just a few stores away.

Fridays and Saturdays were my father's busiest days, in part because Friday was payday and therefore a good day for collecting and Saturday would be a good day both for collecting and selling because of the many customers who would be home rather than working. These would be 12 to 14 hour days of work. Sunday was a day of rest and the car was used to make visits to family, primarily my various aunts and uncles, and to my father's parents while they were still alive.

As the business developed, I began to get to know some of the customers myself. I certainly remember the Breux family he refers to, for Madame Breux (as my father also notes) reminded one of the Madame Plouffe character from the popular Quebec-based situation TV comedy series La Famille Plouffe, which was very popular during the 1950s. One customer, a Mr. Maisonneuve, became a good friend who helped my father at times when he was ill by driving my mother around to help with the collecting before I was old enough to drive myself.

When I was older and could drive I collected for my father when he was ill and couldn't do it himself. On these occasions I was usually accompanied by my mother or friends, including Barbara, my future wife. Since most of my father's customers were French Canadians, I would use my best schoolboy French to mention his name and to say that I was collecting for him. On one occasion I recall that the person who answered the door didn't seem to recognize my father's name. When he finally realized who I was referring to he said, "Oh, you mean the little Jew." While this exchange may not have been representative of all of my father's customers, it did give me a perspective on how he was perceived by at least some of them. I also realized that while he rarely complained about his work, he must have had a difficult time compromising his socialist ideals to earn his living in a manner reminiscent of the type of work that characterized the petty business activity of generations of Jews before him.

I know that when he finally retired, a gradual process that involved little or no new sales and collecting that which was owed to him over a number of years, he rarely referred to his days as an installment merchant. However, he realized that this phase of his life involved an interesting aspect of the Jewish history of Montreal. I am pleased that he included this chapter in his memoirs and I am not aware of any other description of this particular niche of business activity that was common when I was growing up.

Epilogue

As I mentioned in the foreword, the memoirs that my father and mother wrote in Yiddish continued to describe their lives through their retirement years until shortly before their deaths. My father translated two more chapters beyond Chapter 7, the last one of this chronicle. The Yiddish version has a total of 12 chapters. However, the vast majority of these later descriptions detailed family developments that were, to my mind, less interesting than the earlier events that my parents refer to. As my parents aged, and as I became more involved in their care, I became a part of what has been called "the sandwich generation," a situation no different than that of millions of other North American families. Moreover, since the events that were described were often ones that I participated in myself, my memory did not always coincide exactly with my father's. As with many other families there were stresses and strains, particularly in the years shortly before my mother and father passed away. I noticed that my father was beginning to inject his feelings and biases on these points into his writing as he continued to edit and translate these memoirs after my mother passed away. I decided that Chapter 7 was a good place to stop, and I think he understood and realized that there was no point in continuing the translating.

Both of my parents came from sizable families. My father was the youngest of seven children, while my mother was the second youngest of eight. My sister, my only surviving sibling, was almost 10 years older than I was. Hence, I grew up with a large number of older cousins, and family gatherings often involved a substantial number of relatives. In the chapter dealing with the Adath Israel Congregation (Chapter 6), my father mentions that it was expected that my sister's wedding and my Bar Mitzvah would be held in that institution. And indeed that is what happened. My sister was married there in 1954, and I said my Bar Mitzvah in the Adath Israel sanctuary, in 1957.

My sister Miriam (Mia) was a talented and educated woman who completed a Bachelor of Commerce degree at McGill University and then went on to pass the Chartered Accountancy exam, the only woman out of several hundred men to do so that year. As was common at that time, she married at a young age (19 years) and had four children. Her husband, Alex, was an engineer and meteorologist who worked at a government job until he retired. My parents and I lived in close proximity to my sister and her family until I left Montreal to pursue graduate studies in the United States. Her children, and later my own, were very close to my parents. In her retirement years my sister became an active and respected artist. She passed away after battling cancer in 2007, at the age of 72. Her three daughters, Judy, Gila and Sara, are married and live in Toronto. They have nine children between them. The oldest of my sister's children, David, is not married and lives in Ottawa.

My own story is very much tied up with a move I made with my parents when I was 14 years old. In 1958 we moved to a distant Montreal suburb, l'Abord-a-Plouffe, later part of Chomedey and still later a part of the City of Laval. The move was to the first home that my parents purchased. It was described as a semi-detached duplex in that it consisted of two small homes, one above the other, attached to the identical two small homes. My parents owned one side and another family owned the attached other side. The upper stories of each were rented and the rental income was used to off-set the mortgage costs.

The Werkzieg family lived in the attached duplex and since both ours and theirs were newly constructed, we moved in at about the same time. Our neighbours, Sarna and Leon, were Holocaust survivors. Each survived Auschwitz. They met and married after World War II and they had two daughters, Barbara and Ricki. Barbara, the eldest, was born in Gdansk, Poland in 1946. So Barbara was 12 when I met her. We became best friends and later sweethearts, and we were married in 1967. We spent four years in the United States before settling in Waterloo, Ontario in 1972. Barbara and I had three children, Alisa, Jeremy and Benjamin. All are married and to date, we have five wonderful grandchildren. Sadly, Barbara passed away unexpectedly in September, 2008 as a result of complications from an auto-immune disease.

My father retired gradually from his business as he became older. His approach was to keep collecting what was owed to him, but he stopped selling new merchandise and he did not take on new customers. He was very happy when many of the remaining customers provided him with post-dated cheques so that he didn't have to do as much collecting. In any case, the need for the installment merchant evaporated because of the advent of the credit card world. He and my mother began to spend part of each winter in Miami Beach and that is in fact where the Yiddish version of these memoirs was written.

After their return to Canada from Palestine my parents became involved in various Jewish/Zionist organizations. Usually these were organizations that evolved from the youth movements that are described in Chapter Three. While they were originally ideological and political in nature, they function today primarily as fraternal organizations that raise funds for various philanthropic causes, provide burial plots and organize social events. My parents' reintegration into these organizations was a gradual process, as alluded to earlier. My father became very involved in *Farband*, an organization that developed from the *Poale Zion* movement. My mother was drawn to *Na'amat*, an organization for women dedicated to improving the lives of women and children in Israel and elsewhere. For several years my father also served as secretary of the J.J. Segal Foundation, an organization that provided annual awards for Canadian Jewish literature. The organization was named after J. J. Segal, a noted Canadian Yiddish poet and editor of the *Keneder Adler* (the Canadian Eagle), the primary Canadian Yiddish newspaper. My father's main role was to act as an interface between the authors who were nominated for awards and the adjudicators. As someone who never went to high school, and certainly not to college or university, my father revelled in this activity.

As they aged, my parents' health began to deteriorate, particularly my mother's. She suffered from severe osteoporosis. In her mid 70s she fell and broke her shoulder. An effort to repair the damage surgically was not successful and she was forced to take steroids for the rest of her life. My father was her devoted champion and attendant until she died in 1996, after a marriage of 61 years.

My father's translating efforts regarding his and my mother's memoirs continued after my mother's death. In addition, he became interested and concerned with organized Jewish life in Canada, particularly with respect to whether the Jewish leadership was democratically chosen. While he considered himself to be a religious Jew in the traditional sense, he also regretted what he saw as the demise of secular Jewish life in Canada and elsewhere. He became involved, to a modest extent, in the politics of the Canadian Jewish Congress, and he wrote a number of letters on these topics to the editors of tabloids and newspapers such as the Canadian Jewish News. Most of these writing efforts were in English and I was happy to provide editing assistance.

After my mother's death, my father realized that it was time to move closer to his immediate family. I live in Waterloo, Ontario and, as noted, my sister's three daughters live in Toronto. In addition, my sister moved from Montreal to Peterborough, Ontario. Another deciding factor was the infamous ice storm that affected Montreal during the winter of 1998. During the storm my father was forced to evacuate his apartment. Fortunately, he was able to ride out the storm at the home of one of my cousins. And so in the summer of 1998 my father left Montreal, his home since his return from Palestine in the late 1930s, to start a new life in Toronto at the age of 89.

My father flourished in Toronto. He made a number of new friends, had an active social and cultural life and of course there was family nearby. He visited Waterloo often. Several of the letter writing efforts I referred to earlier emanated from his apartment in Toronto. My father lived an independent life until the spring of 2002 when he suffered a massive stroke that left him largely paralyzed. He died in hospital three weeks later after having just turned 93 years of age.

My father continued to feel that he was a *chalutz*, a pioneer, even after he left Palestine. I believe that this is one of the main points of this memoir. He felt that he was a *chalutz* in his job as a building superintendent, and in his work as an installment merchant and in the way he dealt with the trials and tribulations of his retirement years. And his move from Montreal to Toronto at the age of 89 was certainly a courageous decision, one that he made not only for himself but also for his family. I know this since I was one of the major beneficiaries of his move.

About a year or so before he died, my father was still immersed in thoughts and concerns related to the continued existence of the Jewish people. He felt that there was an important need for an ideological renewal and a new Jewish sense of purpose. He wrote up a list of objectives for a new Jewish organization and I helped, as usual, by doing the editing. The list is as follows, exactly as he worded it:

Canadian Jewish Movement

1. *The existence and security of the State of Israel is the supreme feature of Jewish existence.*

2. *Our main aim is to preserve modern Jewish culture in Hebrew, Yiddish, English and other languages.*

3. *Jewish education, both for children and adults, is our primary activity.*

4. *We stand for honest social democracy in Jewish life, on the same level and pattern as Canadian democracy.*

5. *We are committed to maintain a pluralistic approach to the traditions of Judaism.*

6. *We intend to serve our members' traditional burial needs with modesty and simplicity.*

7. *We are committed to an enlightened Jewish Canadian lifestyle, which includes song, dance and friendship.*

8. *The new organizational drive will be based on localities and not on existing branch organizations.*

9. *Please, Jewish men and women of all ages, join our ranks.*

10. *For further information please call the following numbers:*